"The Lookout on the Watch Tower"

In over fifty years of critical appraising Howells frequently welcomed writers now forgotten—who today reads a novel of Henry Ward Beecher?—and occasionally failed fully to appreciate writers acclaimed by a later generation, such as Whitman and Melville. But he held out a welcoming hand to so many young writers when they stood most in need of support that one has no difficulty in understanding why he came at last to be known as the Dean of American letters. "How truly generous and humane is the Dean of American Letters," wrote Theodore Dreiser, who in 1900 as a young reporter interviewed the established novelist and critic. Dreiser added, "The great literary philanthropist, I call him." A genuine pleasure in the flash of truth in the writing of another made Howells recognize at once the power of Mark Twain, the red-headed stranger from the West who shocked literary Boston by his irreverencies; enabled him to welcome Bret Harte to his Cambridge home in spite of his swaggering pretensions; moved him to urge the publishing of Henry James's stories in the Atlantic *when Fields hesitated; impelled him to walk from publisher to publisher with a privately printed copy of Stephen Crane's* Maggie *in his hand and to write the first American review of it when the book finally was published in England. Howells was, in Dreiser's words, "the lookout on the watch tower straining for a glimpse of approaching genius."*

—from the Introduction

WILLIAM DEAN HOWELLS

EUROPEAN
AMERICAN

AND
MASTERS

Edited with Introductions by
CLARA MARBURG KIRK and RUDOLF KIRK

COLLIER BOOKS
NEW YORK, N.Y.

This edition, revised for Collier Books, is published by arrangement with New York University Press

Collier Books is a division of The Crowell-Collier Publishing Company

First Collier Books Edition 1963

Library of Congress Catalog Card Number: 62-21363

Hecho en los E. E. U. U.
Printed in the United States of America

Preface

During the past half century few American writers have been so constantly—one is tempted to say so intentionally—misunderstood as William Dean Howells, who in the last quarter of the nineteenth century was regarded by most readers as our foremost man of letters. Various causes for this misunderstanding may be found—social, economic, political, literary, and religious—but the principal one may be that his critical essays have lain hidden in the files of magazines and have been neglected even by most students of our literature. Because these statements of Howells' views and opinions have gone unread, many attitudes and beliefs have been attributed to him that he never harbored and, indeed, explicitly repudiated. It is with the hope that a true conception of Howells' ideas, especially as they concern literature, may be gained by a reading of a substantial selection of his essays that the present volume has been produced. We are not sure that these essays, read alone, would in this day and generation carry their message as they once did. For this reason we have included introductions to explain matters that may be helpful to the present-day reader. But beyond anything we may write about Howells, the student must turn to the sources of the late nineteenth century to understand the background against which he wrote. If he does so, he will go further in correcting common misconceptions than is possible from a mere reading of the essays.

We have attempted, with reasonable fidelity, to adhere to Howells' text in matters of spelling, grammar, and punctuation. A few obvious errors, probably those of typesetters, have been emended in the interest of clarity and consistency. In the notes we have identified only those names and references that cannot be found in such readily available books as *Webster's Collegiate Dictionary* or the *Oxford Companion to English* or the *Oxford Companion to American Literature*.

In the introductions to Howells' essays we have made use of many sources without giving title and page reference. The reason for this seemingly cavalier treatment of the reader is that we have been dependent on so many different writers—both contemporaries of Howells and later students of him and his age—that we should not have known where to insert a reference and where to leave the source to the knowledge of the reader. In general, we are heavily in debt to the three bibliographies compiled by George Arms and William M. Gibson: *A Bibliography of William Dean Howells*, 1948; "Selected Bibliography," in *Representative Selections of William Dean Howells*, edited by the present authors in the "American Writers Series," 1950 (revised 1961); and "Books and Articles on W. D. Howells, 1950-1956," *Howells Sentinel*, Nos. 3 to 6. In addition to these sources, we have of course made use of reference books and magazine and newspaper files.

We wish to thank Professor W. W. Howells of Harvard University for granting us permission to reproduce letters and essays by his grandfather W. D. Howells that are still in copyright. Anyone wishing to make use of this material must secure permission from Professor Howells.

C. M. K.
R. K.

Rutgers University
August, 1962

Introduction

Introduction

For over half a century William Dean Howells profoundly influenced the literary taste of the United States. He helped the American reader recover from a subservient respect for "the classics," especially those of a romantic flavor, by directing his attention to the great realistic writers of Italy, France, Spain, Russia, and the Scandinavian countries. Through editorial columns, first of the *Atlantic Monthly* and then of *Harper's Magazine*, he patiently, humorously, and wisely talked to a widening circle of men and women concerning the importance of truth in literature. As early as 1872 Howells had declared his allegiance to "Real Life" in *Their Wedding Journey*—"Ah, poor Real Life, how I love thy foolish and insipid face." When Howells opened the door of "The Editor's Study" of *Harper's* in January, 1886, he invited his readers, still delighting in the sensational novels of Ouïda and Charles Reade, "to regard our life without the literary glasses so long thought desirable, and to see character, not as it is in other fiction, but as it abounds outside of all fiction."

From 1886 to 1892 Howells' voice became more insistent; every month from "The Editor's Study" it could be heard "perpetually thundering at the gates of Fiction in Error." It is from these *Harper's Magazine* essays that Howells selected the little volume, *Criticism and Fiction*, with which he blasted the "historical romance" before he left his editorial chair in 1892.

Part I of this volume, "European Masters," includes Howells' essays on European writers who helped form his—and our—concept of realism. As a child Howells taught himself not only Latin and Greek, but also German, French, Spanish, and Italian, and was therefore able to profit by his four years abroad as a young consul in Venice and to maintain during all his life an eager interest in the current literature of Europe, where, throughout the century, realism in literature and art developed as an aspect of political and social change. Howells' literary views, published in most of the leading journals of the

day, influenced the literary taste of Americans and drew them
closer to the vast European movement. The eager reading of
European masters that followed suggested to American writers the richness of their native material, realistically conceived.
The Continental novelists teach us to imitate nature, Howells reminded his readers. "Every plant now bearing good and
nourishing fruit" is of that seed, he said. The lesson Howells
learned from his reading of Björnson, Turgenev, Tolstoy, Valdés, Hardy, Zola, and many others was that the greatest
beauty is always associated with the greatest truth. To Howells the "romantic" approach seemed both unethical and unbeautiful. "To be single in the aim to represent life as one has
seen and known and felt it, that is the great thing." Howells'
"literary passions" were wide enough to include poetry and
drama as well as fiction, and to see in Ibsen, for instance, another great advocate of truth in literature, whose purpose was,
like that of the realist in fiction, to understand the impulses of
ordinary people. These European masters, these "literary di-
vinities" who became "the cult of the Study," Howells tire-
lessly interpreted to an American public still reading aloud
Scott, Dickens, and Thackeray.

Part II, "American Writers," reflects the large-minded sympathy that enabled Howells to form a host of associates by
whom he was influenced and whom in turn he influenced. The
list of literary figures is impressive, and to it many more
names could be added. "I knew Hawthorne and Emerson and
Walt Whitman; I knew Longfellow and Holmes and Whittier
and Lowell; I knew Bryant and Bancroft and Motley; I knew
Harriet Beecher Stowe and Julia Ward Howe; I knew Arte-
mus Ward and Stockton and Mark Twain; I knew Parkman
and Fiske," said Howells to the large audience gathered
to celebrate his seventy-fifth birthday. How many more names
and faces must have passed through his mind as he spoke!
For the procession of "literary friends and acquaintance" was
a long one. In over fifty years of critical appraising Howells
frequently welcomed writers now forgotten—who today reads
a novel of Henry Ward Beecher?—and occasionally failed fully
to appreciate writers acclaimed by a later generation, such as
Whitman and Melville. But he held out a welcoming hand to
so many young writers when they stood most in need of sup-

port that one has no difficulty in understanding why he came
at last to be known as the Dean of American Letters. "How
truly generous and humane is the Dean of American Letters,"
wrote Theodore Dreiser, who in 1900 as a young reporter interviewed the established novelist and critic. Dreiser added,
"The great literary philanthropist, I call him." A genuine
pleasure in the flash of truth in the writing of another made
Howells recognize at once the power of Mark Twain, the red-
headed stranger from the West who shocked literary Boston
by his irreverencies; enabled him to welcome Bret Harte to
his Cambridge home in spite of his swaggering pretensions;
moved him to urge the publishing of Henry James's stories in
the *Atlantic* when Fields hesitated; impelled him to walk
from publisher to publisher with a privately printed copy of
Stephen Crane's *Maggie* in his hand and to write the first
American review of it when the book finally was published in
England. Howells was, in Dreiser's words, " 'the lookout on
the watch tower' straining for a first glimpse of approaching
genius." Perhaps because Howells was himself both a novelist
and a critic, he took a peculiar delight in his editorial contact
with young writers: "I do not know how it is with other editors who are also authors," he wrote, "but I can truly say for
myself that nothing of my own which I thought fresh and
true ever gave me more pleasure than that I got from the
like qualities in the work of some young writer revealing his
power."

Contents

Part II: AMERICAN WRITERS

PART I: EUROPEAN MASTERS

Introduction

In Part I* of this volume we have gathered some of the essays and reviews of William Dean Howells on European writers of the second half of the nineteenth century. These not only show the working of his singularly clear and sensitive mind, but serve also as examples of how he educated a generation of American readers in the great realistic writers of fiction then appearing in Europe.

Soon after Howells joined the staff of the *Atlantic Monthly* in 1866, he became friendly with an obscure young contributor named Henry James, and through him he met Thomas Sergeant Perry, a Harvard tutor in French and German from 1868 to 1872, and then for two years editor of the *North American Review*. Under Perry's guidance Howells' range of reading and reviewing was widened to include the writers of Italy, Spain, France, Russia, Germany, and the Scandinavian countries. In "Recollections of an Atlantic Editorship," written for the fiftieth anniversary of the *Atlantic* in November, 1907, Howells tells us with his customary candor that "to the reviews of American and English books I added certain pages of notices of French and German literature, and in these I had the very efficient and singularly instructed help of Mr. Thomas Sergeant Perry, who knew not only more of current continental literature than any other American, but more than all other Americans." The new department was called "Recent Literature," and Perry was commissioned to contribute to it when Howells assumed the editorship of the *Atlantic* in January, 1871.

Howells' early reviews of European writers in the *Atlantic* reflect his response to the winds of realism blowing across Europe at a time when most Americans were still engaged with Scott (who, Howells asserted, built pasteboard castles), and Dickens (who, according to Howells, thought he felt more

* The notes to Part I begin on p. 219.

deeply than he actually did), and Thackeray (who, Howells claimed, was a trickster).

One has only to reread the early chapters of his retrospective book *My Literary Passions* (1895) to realize that Howells, as a hungry reader of the classics in Ohio, had "given his heart" to each of these giants in turn—and to many another in the "Bookcase at Home." That Howells never forgot these early enthusiasms, even after he recognized the limitations of his favorites, is reflected in portions of an essay he wrote for *Munsey's Magazine* (April, 1897), with which Part I begins.

Now, however, these English authors were swept aside in order to give place to the new and dazzling writers from Europe whom Howells read with eager attention, sometimes before their novels were translated, and introduced to his readers first through the *Atlantic Monthly* and later through *Harper's Weekly, Harper's Monthly, Literature,* the *North American Review,* and many other papers and magazines. Not only did the stories of Björnson, Turgenev, Hardy (the only living English novelist whom Howells consistently admired), Verga, Valdés, Galdós, Zola, and Tolstoy affect Howells' own technique as a writer, but they became for him the standard-bearers of the new realistic movement in novel writing. A reading of Howells' appraisals of these writers as they first appeared in leading American magazines helps us to understand that realism was to Howells much more than a literary movement; it was, in fact, a fresh approach to truth itself, and it held for him an important social implication.

Howells' extraordinary grasp of the new fiction which poured across his editorial desk, and which he discussed with the writers and authors who passed through his office, would not have been possible had he not been himself a linguist. *Years of My Youth* (1916) gives the reader a moving account of Howells' boyish "struggle with those alien languages." The importance to the future critic of the knowledge of these languages was the reading of many writers in the original—Cervantes, Ariosto, Dante, Schiller, Goldoni, and others—that Howells managed to crowd into his early days as a printer and a reporter in Ohio and into his years in Venice.

Howells later regretted the time he had spent in his lonely

youth studying these languages and poring over his well-thumbed classics. As an older man, looking back at the literary passions of a self-taught boy, he wished he had seen "more of the actual world" and had learned to know his "brethren in it better." However, it was because of his knowledge of languages that he was able to escape from the drudgery of the family newspaper. His mastery of German led him to apply for a consulship in Munich; when he actually received an appointment to Venice he knew enough Italian to accept it; his understanding of French gave him an early acquaintance with Zola, Flaubert, Maupassant, Daudet, and others; his reading of the Spanish classics helped him to grasp the importance of Armando Palacio Valdés in his own tradition. Most important of all, through first-hand acquaintance with the Continental novelists Howells was moved to question the supremacy of English fiction, to give impetus to the study of European novels in this country, and through his understanding of these writers to encourage the early signs of "the new spirit" in American writers.

For Howells hoped to relate American fiction, which he freely admitted to be very uneven in its performance, to the "only living movement in imaginative literature," that of the Continental novelists. "The disposition to regard life without the literary glasses so long thought desirable," which he saw in the best of our writers, "distinguishes by a superior freshness and authenticity any group of American novels from a similarly accidental group of English novels, giving them the same good right to be as the like number of recent Russian novels, French novels, Spanish novels, Italian novels, Norwegian novels."

In the essay in *Munsey's Magazine* written in 1897 Howells, still encouraging the "new spirit" wherever he discerns it, admits quite candidly that "if you had a vote of the critics in the United States today, it would declare by a large majority for the romantic novel." He is, however, impressed by the growing popularity of such a writer as Henry B. Fuller, whose realistic picture of Chicago in *The Cliff Dwellers* (1893) makes the author "very distinctly part of the future." Fuller and other young writers of his decade give Howells hope that taste is turning away from the crudely romantic in fiction. "A prodigious impulse in every direction . . . in the arts as well as in affairs" was felt in this country after the Civil War, Howells declares, when American writers, like the realistic writers of Europe, began to do "new things." In Part II of this book we shall see which American writers seemed important and what "new things" they were doing. Although "the yoke of England" is still felt in criticism, Howells observes, "American fiction is as free as it can very well be. We do not take the word from anybody." With an optimistic prophecy—"I should say that America was still coming in fiction"—Howells waves us on to the future.

Part I concerns the European masters whom for a quarter of a century Howells had been introducing to American readers. Each in his way reflected the new interest in the inner lives of ordinary people and thus unconsciously added a new dimension to a definition of realism that Howells helped to establish in American fiction.

We have preserved the spellings of proper names within quotations, though we have used the modern spellings in our own introductions.

Dickens and Thackeray

In *Criticism and Fiction* (1891) Howells said it is the critic's business "to break the images of false gods and misshapen heroes, to take away the poor silly toys that many grown people would still like to play with." These toys were, of course, the "heroes" and "heroines," moved by "the old romantic ideals," and the malevolent villains, quite as false to ordinary experience.

To Howells, realism was "nothing more and nothing less than the truthful treatment of material"; one is not surprised, then, to read that "the divine Jane" is "alone worthy to be matched with the great Scandinavian and Slavic and Latin artists." Howells wrote: "Because of the mania of romanticism, the art of fiction, as Jane Austen knew it, declined from her through Scott, and Bulwer, and Dickens, and Charlotte Brontë, and Thackeray, and even George Eliot." This mania seized upon all Europe in the nineteenth century; England, however, has shown few signs of recovery, in spite of the example of a subtle use of realism in the Continental masterpieces at her door. George Eliot and Thomas Hardy, to be sure, break through the fog of "those poor islanders," but they avail little since English criticism has continued "provincial, and special and personal."

Howells' choice of adjectives seems to have been vindicated by the storm of comment that *Criticism and Fiction* elicited from the British critics immediately after its appearance in 1891. Andrew Lang in the *Illustrated London News* of April 1, 1891, records:

> The friends of romance pray daily, but almost without hope, for the conversion of Mr. W. D. Howells. At this hour he is impenitent, and the best we can hope for is that his is a case of "invincible ignorance." Mr. Howells is not content with monthly blaspheming against romance in the magazine of Messrs. Harper. He has reproduced a variety of his remarks in a little volume, "Criticism and Fiction."

23

In the next issue of the *Illustrated London News* William Archer takes Howells to task for "the injudicious vivacity of expression" that leads him to overstate his case for realism in *Criticism and Fiction,* the "main contentions" of which "the unprejudiced observer" is forced to accept. The critic writing in the *Literary World* of June 20, 1891, treats the author of the provocative little volume with less tenderness. Many of Howells' dicta, he commented, "are as entertaining and instructive as the judgments of a Pawnee brave in the galleries of the Louvre would be."

Howells' attack on British critics and British novelists could not have been a complete surprise to the English, for the battle had been joined in 1882 when Howells inserted several telling paragraphs in his essay "Henry James, Jr." written for the November *Century.* Before Howells sailed for England after his resignation from the *Atlantic,* the essay was left with Richard Watson Gilder, the new editor of the *Century.* Howells and his family spent a happy summer in London, seeing many English and American friends, before setting forth for Switzerland in September. The first intimation of the stir that Howells' latest essay caused in London came to him in a letter from Henry James written from London in November, 1882. He too had been out of London when the *Century* arrived, and thus "I missed the little breeze produced, as I am told, by the November Century." Mildred Howells reports in *Life in Letters* that the paragraphs referring to Dickens and Thackeray "brought a storm of abuse upon Howells from people who probably did not understand what he had said." The reader of today understands more fully than the reader of 1882 possibly could the significance of the statement imbedded in Howells' essay, "Henry James, Jr.," for we read it with the light cast upon the whole controversy by *Criticism and Fiction.* Howells reports that the offending sentences, reprinted below, caused much "skull-cracking."

> The art of fiction has, in fact, become a finer art in our day than it was with Dickens and Thackeray. We could not suffer the confidential attitude of the latter now, or the mannerism of the former, any more than we could endure the prolixity of Richardson or the coarseness of Fielding.

These great men are of the past—they and their methods and interests; even Trollope and Reade are not of the present. The new school derives from Hawthorne and George Eliot rather than any others; but it studies human nature much more in its wonted aspects, and finds its ethical and dramatic examples in the operation of lighter but not really less vital motives. The moving accident is certainly not its trade; and it prefers to avoid all manner of dire catastrophes. It is largely influenced by French fiction in form; but it is the realism of Daudet rather than the realism of Zola that prevails with it, and it has a soul of its own which is above the business of recording the rather brutish pursuit of a woman by a man, which seems to be the chief end of the French novelist. This school, which is so largely of the future as well as the present, finds its chief exemplar in Mr. James; it is he who is shaping and directing American fiction, at least.

Though Howells had not received the November *Century* in Switzerland, he had heard of the excitement his comments had caused among the English. To Roswell Smith, the new owner of the *Century*, he wrote at once:

I suppose you will have seen that I have stirred up the English papers pretty generally by what I wrote of Dickens and Thackeray in my paper on James. I don't remember just what I said, but so far as they have quoted me, I stand by myself, and should only wish to amplify and intensify the opinions that they object to. I knew what I was talking about, and they don't know at all what they are talking about.

To Edmund Gosse he wrote that he would like to "say [his] say of D. & T.," but, he added, "I am far too lazy and too busy to see the hour of doing it." Howells seized his chance to say his say in answer to "the English clamor" when he took over "The Editor's Study" of *Harper's* in 1886. His rejection of the worn-out novel techniques of Dickens and Thackeray became an essential aspect of his espousal of the new and subtler techniques of the European masters to whom

he had been turning during his *Atlantic* period. A sense of
how an interest in the Continental writers was connected in
James's mind as well as in Howells' with a repudiation of the
English novels and of "romantic phantoms" in their own aims
as novelists is to be found in a letter written February 21,
1884, by James in Paris to his friend Howells in Boston.
James, after reporting that "I have been seeing something of
Daudet, Goncourt, and Zola," refers to "the floods of tepid
soap and water which under the name of novels are being
vomited forth in England," and adds: "I say this to you because I regard you as the great American naturalist. I don't
think you go far enough, and you are haunted with romantic
phantoms and a tendency to factitious glosses; but you are on
the right path and I wish you repeated triumphs."

That readers of the period recognized the importance of
the attack on the accepted pillars of the English novel, Dickens and Thackeray, is attested by an article by Maurice
Thompson in the Philadelphia *Book News* of November,
1887. After an opening paragraph on Howells' early life
and his work on the *Atlantic,* Thompson observed that Howells, before the publication of his *Century* essay on James, was
"practically unknown in England":

In November, 1882, was published in the *Century Magazine* Mr. Howells' sketch of Henry James, in which he set
forth his critical opinion of Charles Dickens, stating in
effect that he considered Henry James a greater artist and a
better novelist than either Thackeray or Dickens. No doubt
Mr. Howells was as much surprised as anybody else when
the English critics attacked him and his little essay with a
suddenness and acrimony wholly unlooked for. The result
was two-fold: at once Mr. Howells and Mr. James, having
gained British attention, stepped to the front of American
interest. By what the English critics deemed unmitigated
audacity, Mr. Howells had set himself and his method of
novel-writing over against the personality and the method
of the greatest English romancer since Scott. The situation
was one that not even Hawthorne's genius had ever com-
manded. British resentment was quite sufficient to awaken

American attention—it always is. Mr. Howells saw his opportunity and threw the whole force of his talent into an effort to profit by it. But here again, as always, he kept himself well in hand. The situation did not change the current of his development, it merely hastened its flow. He began to attack romance and to set himself forward as the spokesman of the realistic "school" in American fiction. If, as a critic, he has fallen far short of greatness, he has succeeded in attracting wide attention, and has made his position an anomalous and interesting one. Chiefly, in this regard, he has chosen to be the enthusiastic, even headstrong, eulogist of Tolstoi, and, recently, of Zola.

That Howells stood firmly by his opinions in his critical reading of his two old favorites, Dickens and Thackeray, is evident not only in his comments on these novelists in *Criticism and Fiction*, but also in the brief excerpt presented below from a long essay he wrote for *Munsey's Magazine* in April, 1897, entitled "My Favorite Novelist and His Best Book." At the request of the editor, Howells as a member of a symposium of writers, here tells of the development of his literary taste. One is not surprised to discover that "the favorite novelist" at that time was Tolstoy, nor is one unprepared to learn that there have been a great many "favorite novelists" in the literary development of this omnivorous reader, then in his sixtieth year. Howells' recovery from the enthusiasms of his youth, so winningly traced in *My Literary Passions* just two years before the publication of the following essay, reflects his "changed point of view" that turned him from the "potent charm" of Dickens and the "worldly pride" of Thackeray to the truer claim of the writers of Europe. These Continental novelists, without any apparent artifice, bring one to an understanding of the inner life of ordinary people. *My Literary Passions*, Howells' autobiography as a reader (abbreviated in "My Favorite Novelist"), contains a still fuller account of his abiding love of the novels of Dickens and Thackeray. But their heroes and heroines, not to mention their villains, were undoubtedly "poor silly toys," to be cherished only in sentimental moments by a responsible critic conscious of the new voices of psychological realism from Europe.

MY FAVORITE NOVELIST AND HIS BEST BOOK*

To say something concerning novels, and particularly of my favorite among them? That is a difficult thing to do, for one's point of view changes so much from youth to middle age. One's favorite at twenty would not be one's favorite later; but I am pretty sure that throughout my life there has been an increasing preference for what seems to me *real* in fiction as against what seems to me *factitious*; and whilst I have been very fond, from time to time, of the pure romance, I have never cared for the romantic novel, since I was very young.

I used to be extremely fond of what, perhaps, was a pretty true picture of life in its way—"Handy Andy." It was one of the first novels I read, and it was an early favorite with me; and then I read others of Lover and Lever—their names are so much alike that I confound their novels as well. But before that I had favorite novels: the Indian and pioneer romances of Emerson Bennett, and, the very first of all, a story of Lowell's friend, George F. Briggs [Charles F. Briggs], called "The Trippings of Tom Pepper"—I fancy still a pretty good story, though it is fifty years since I read it. It was not necessary, then, however, that a novel should be good in order to be my favorite. In fact, I am rather surprised that "Don Quixote" should have been my favorite about the same time, and that Poe's tales should have been equally my favorites.

As a boy, I liked Captain Marryatt's novels ever so much. I have not read any of them since except "Jacob Faithful"; I read that about ten years ago, and was very much amused to find what hard reading it was, though as a boy I had found it so easy. All this may illustrate what I mean by a changed point of view.

Later, of course, I read Dickens, and with most passionate liking, for a long time. Within a little while past I have read a good part of "Our Mutual Friend," "Bleak House," and "Dav-

* *Munsey's Magazine,* April, 1897.

id Copperfield," and liked them still, but not with the old, or
young ardor. You are always aware in Dickens, how he is
"making it up," but he was a great master;[1] and I suppose
that "David Copperfield" is his most representative book,
though there are some of his later novels, like the "Tale of
Two Cities," which are more shapely; but the English custom
of novel publication was always against form, against balance. Dickens issued his novels, until he started *Household
Words,* in numbers; George Eliot published hers in the same
way, and I believe wrote them from month to month as they
appeared, as Mr. Hardy still writes his. A novel was not completed when its publication began. In fact, from number to
number the author hardly knew what was going to happen. In
a letter to Forster, Dickens tells that he was once in a sta-
tioner's shop when a lady came in and asked whether a certain number of "David Copperfield" was out; it was to be the
next, and he hadn't put pen to paper, or even imagined it fully.
Such conditions are fatal to symmetry. But they were the
economic conditions. That was the way the author could best
make his living, and the way an artist can best make his living
always tells upon his art. . . .

The novelist who was my favorite all through my early
manhood was Thackeray, whom I don't now think the great
artist I then did; indeed, I find him very much less an artist
than Dickens. The plots of Dickens, to be sure, are not such
as come out of his characters. The true plot comes out of the
character; that is, the man does not result from the things he
does, but the things he does result from the man, and so plot
comes out of character; plot aforethought does not charac-
terize. But Dickens believed it did, and all the romantic
school of writers believed it did. Bulwer, Charles Reade, and
even George Eliot, in some measure, thought so; but for all
that—all that faking, that useless and false business of creating
a plot and multiplying incidents—Dickens was the greater artist, because he could somehow make the thing transact itself. He got it to stand upon its legs and walk off. Thackeray is
always holding his figures up from behind, and commenting
upon them, and explaining them. In the midst of his narration
he stops and writes little essays about his characters. That is
the business of the critic, not the novelist. The business of the

novelist is to put certain characters before you, and keep them before you, with as little of the author apparent as possible. In a play the people have no obvious interference from the author at all. Of course he creates them, but there is no comment; there can be none. The characters do it all. The novelist who carried the play method furthest is Tourguénief, and for a long time I preferred him to any other; he was the first Russian novelist I read, and on my revulsion from Thackeray, Tourguénief became my greatest favorite.

The novels of incident, of adventure, do not interest me. But I do not believe their authors write simply for popularity, or for the moment. I believe they do the thing they like to do; but the thing they do is worthless, as far as I am concerned. I am not sure that I am quite logical in not caring for novels of adventure, for I am very fond of the circus, and like to see people flying through the air; and I would go to a fire, any day.

As to what I once said about our not being able to throw off the yoke of England intellectually, although we had long ago done so politically, I did not mean so much our fiction as our criticism. American fiction is as free as it can very well be. We do not take the word from anybody; but English taste influences our criticism. If you had a vote of the critics in the United States today, it would declare by a large majority for the romantic novel, which is distinctly a second rate novel, judging it by the quality of the men who produce it. It would be the same in England, where the novel of that sort continues to be taken seriously, though there is no other country in Europe where it could possibly be taken seriously. But the English are so far behind that they prefer a novel of that sort. They are a very romantic people. . . .

Bjornstjerne Bjornson (1832—1910)

Howells tells us in *My Literary Passions* that during a long illness soon after he went to live in Cambridge, he read with delight translations of the first three of Björnstjerne Björnson's novels to appear in this country, *Arne* (1869), *The Happy Boy* (1870), and *The Fisher-Maiden* (1869). The young editor soon included his appraisal of these stories in "Reviews and Literary Notices" for the *Atlantic Monthly* and thus helped to establish Björnson's reputation in the United States. So rapidly did an appreciation of his novels grow that by 1890 all his works had appeared in translation. Well known in his day as novelist, poet, playwright, and essayist, Björnson is now almost forgotten; but between 1870 and his death he was considered the herald of a new school of writing.

When Howells wrote his review of Björnson's three novels for the *Atlantic* he had not met the Norwegian and knew little of him as a political figure in his own country. Howells himself was at that time the author of several slim books of poetry and travel; he was attending the great Longfellow's Dante evenings; he was lecturing on Italian literature at Harvard College; and he was industriously writing reviews for the *Atlantic*. But the recent success of *Italian Journeys*, which was crowded with realistic pictures of Italian streets and Italian characters in the Goldoni tradition, had set Howells' imagination to work on the problems of a fiction writer as well as on those of a critic. It was as both a critic and an aspiring novelist that he read Björnson's stories. To waste no words on elaborate description, to present one's characters briefly, and then to let the plot flow naturally from the characters—that was to achieve the dramatic effect that charmed Howells, first in Björnson and later in Turgenev. Both novelists managed to stay close to the truth, avoiding the style of the French naturalists and of the "blond romances" then flooding the market.

In Björnson's novels Howells found the blend of poetry and

31

realism for which he himself was searching and which he was
soon to express in *Their Wedding Journey, A Chance Acquaintance,* and many other novels. In a brief comment on
The Railroad and the Churchyard, by Björnson, in the *Atlantic* of November, 1870, Howells pointed out with approval
that the realistically treated characters are "as exquisitely
painted as any ideal figure" because they are "humble but decent folk" seen through the eyes of a poet who at the same
time is true to his simple Norwegian background. Though the
reader is aware that he is reading romance, Howells said, he
feels that the author presents the truth of the real as well as of
the ideal in these stories. Howells learned from Björnson that
"the finest poetry is not ashamed of the plainest fact," and he
found in the Norwegian's novels the romance of real life,
which he carried over to his own stories. "He has my love,"
wrote Howells in *My Literary Passions,* "not only because he
is a poet of the most exquisite verity, but because he is a lover
of men, with a faith in them such as can move mountains of
ignorance, and dullness, and greed."

When Björnson came to the United States on a lecture tour
in 1880-1881, Howells lunched with the "poet" (he does
not call him novelist) and recognized him again as a
"great genius." For almost thirty years Björnson and Howells
read each other's novels and corresponded intermittently.
Howells tells us that when he saw "the great Norwegian"
again in 1908, Björnson knew him at once and met him
"with both hands out, and 'My dear, dear Howells!' " Miss
Howells adds, in an editorial note to Howells' letter describing
the occasion, that "the two saw each other often in Rome,
Björnson towering majestically over Howells at their meetings, for he was a giant physically as well as mentally."

Both Howells and Björnson turned to social problems for
subjects for their novels in the 1890's. In "The Editor's
Study" of *Harper's Monthly* of February, 1887, Howells
refers to "that colossus of the North"; one cannot but specu-
late as to the indebtedness of Howells' *Rise of Silas Lapham*
(1885) to Björnson's play *The Bankrupt* (1874), a translation of which Howells might have read in French or German. In "The Editor's Study" of February, 1889, he points
out that the conditions shown in this play are as familiar in

the United States as in Norway. He refers to Björnson as "next to Tolstoy in his willingness to give himself for his kind." In his review of Björnson's novel *In God's Way*, in *Harper's*, February, 1891, Howells notes that his "entirely human characters" are seriously concerned with "matters of conscience," and that the reader is not "trifled with or defrauded by any trick of the trade in any part of the action," for Björnson is concerned with the truth and "never fails of reality on the high level his imagination keeps." If one compares Maupassant's *Notre Coeur* with Björnson's novel, says Howells, he will see how "the Frenchman grovels into mere romanticism and is false even to the fashionable filth he studies." Naturalism and romanticism are aspects of the same movement; true realism, as exemplified by Björnson, stays close to the "never-failing springs" of ordinary life and is not afraid to reflect the element of poetry that surrounds the commonplace. Howells summed up Björnson's place in the realistic movement ("The Editor's Study," February, 1889) as "a foremost one, though his realism is of the spiritual type, like that of the Russians, rather than the sensual type, like that of the French, . . . for he is, above all, a poet, . . . one of the chief of those great Norsemen of our time who have led their poetry back not only to the life but to the language of the people."

Reproduced below is the essay on the stories of Björnson that Howells wrote for the *Atlantic* in 1870. His summaries of the stories are omitted. In this review of the recently translated tales Howells is not only actually introducing a new writer to the reader, but he is also suggesting his own evolving ideas on novel writing. Almost all the critical beliefs that he defined more sharply in *Criticism and Fiction* are to be found in this early essay, as well as implied definitions of such terms as romance, naturalism, and realism.

NORWEGIAN ROMANCES*

The author of that unique essay, "The Glut of the Fiction Market,"[2] who had the good fortune to put more truth about

novels into wittier phrase than any other essayist of this time,
held that having exhausted all the types and situations and
catastrophes of English fiction, we must give it up as a source
of literary amusement; and, indeed, there are very few critics
who do not now, in their heart of hearts (if they have any),
secretly look forward to a time when people shall read nothing but book-notices.

Whilst this millennial period is still somewhat distant, their
weariness of our own novelists is attested by nothing so vividly
as the extraordinary welcome which has of late been given to
translations of the novels of all other races; for, generally
speaking, these invaders of our realm of fiction are not better
than the novelists they have displaced, but only different.
Miss Mühlbach,[3] the author of a vast, and, we believe, increasing horde of blond romances, is the most formidable foe
that our sorrier sort of fictionists have had to contend with,
and in her train have followed unnumbered others, though
none so popular and so poor. Amongst these, indeed, have
appeared several of striking merit, and conspicuously Björnstjerne Björnson, the Norwegian whose beautiful romances we
wish all our readers to like with us. Concerning the man himself, we know little more than that he is the son of a country
clergyman, and that, after a rather unpromising career in
school and college, he has risen to the first place in the literature of the North, and has almost invented a new pleasure in
the fresh and wonderful tales he writes about Norwegian life.
He has been the manager of a theatre, and he has written
many plays, but we believe he is known in English only by the
three books of which we have given the titles below, and
which form an addition to literature of as great and certain
value as any which has been otherwise made during the last
two years.

There is in the way the tales are told a singular simplicity,
or a reticence and self-control that pass for this virtue, and

---

* *Arne*: *A Sketch of Norwegian Country Life,* translated by
Augusta Plesner and S. Rugeley Powers, 1866. *The Happy Boy*:
A Tale of Norwegian Peasant Life, translated by H. R. G., 1870.
The Fisher-Maiden: *A Norwegian Tale.* From the author's German
edition, by M. E. Niles, 1869. Reviewed in the *Atlantic Monthly*,
April, 1870.

that take the aesthetic sense as winningly as their sentiment touches the heart. The author has entire confidence in his reader's intelligence. He believes, it seems, that we can be fully satisfied with a few distinct touches in representing a situation or a character; he is the reverse, in a word, of all that is Trollopian in literary art. He does not concern himself with detail, nor with general statement, but he makes some one expressive particular serve for all introduction and explanation of a fact. The life he portrays is that, for the most part, of humble but decent folk; and this choice of subject is also novel and refreshing in contrast with the subjects of our own fictions, in which there seems to be no middle ground between magnificent drawing-rooms and the most unpleasant back-alleys, or between very refined and well-born company and the worst reprobates of either sex. How much of our sense of his naturalness would survive further acquaintance with Björnson we cannot venture to say; the conventionalities of a literature are but too perilously apt to be praised as *naïveté* by foreign criticism, and we have only the internal evidence that peasant-boys like Arne, and fisher-maidens like Petra, are not as common and tiresome in Norwegian fiction as we find certain figures in our own novels. We would willingly celebrate them, therefore, with a wise reserve, and season our delight with doubt, as a critic should; though we are not at all sure that we can do this. . . .

With people in another rank, Charles Reade would have managed this as charmingly, though he would have thrown into it somewhat too much of the brilliancy of the footlights; and Auerbach would have done it with equal naturalness; but neither could have cast about it that poetic atmosphere which is so peculiarly the gift of Björnson and of the Northern mind, and which is felt in its creations, as if the glamour of the long summer days of the North had got into literature. It is very noticeable throughout "Arne." The facts are stated with perfect ruggedness and downrightness when necessary, but some dreamy haze seems still to cling about them, subduing their hard outlines and features like the tender light of the slanting Norwegian sun on the craggy Norwegian headlands. The romance is interspersed with little lyrics, pretty and graceful in their form, but of just the quality to show that Björnson is

wise to have chosen prose for the expression of his finer and
stronger thoughts.

In that region of novel characters, wholesome sympathies,
and simple interests to which he transports us, we have not
only a blissful sense of escape from the jejune inventions and
stock repetitions of what really seems a failing art with us,
but are aware of our contact with an excellent and enviable
civilization. Of course the reader sees the Norwegians and
their surroundings through Björnson's poetic eyes, and is
aware that he is reading romance; yet he feels that there must
be truth to the real as well as the ideal in these stories.

"Arne" is the most poetical of the three, and the action is
principally in a world where the troubles are from within, and
inherent in human nature, rather than from any artificial
causes, though the idyllic sweetness is chiefly owing to the circumstances of the characters as peasant-folk in a "North
countree." In "The Happy Boy" the world of conventions and
distinctions is more involved by the fortunes of the lovers; for
the happy boy Oeyvind is made wretched enough in the good
old way by finding out that there is a difference between riches
and poverty in the eyes of grandparents, at least, and he is tor-
mented in his love of Marit by his jealousy of a wealthier rival. It is Marit's worldly and ambitious grandfather who for-
bids their love, and will have only unpleasant things to say to
Oeyvind, until the latter comes back from the Agricultural
College, and establishes himself in his old home with the re-
pute of the best farmer in the neighborhood. Meantime unre-
mitted love-making goes on between Marit and Oeyvind,
abetted by Oeyvind's schoolmaster, through whom indeed all
their correspondence was conducted while Oeyvind was away
at school. At last the affair is happily concluded when Ole
Nordistuen, the grandfather, finds that his farm is going to
ruin, and nothing can save it but the skill of Oeyvind.

In this story the peasant life is painted in a more naturalistic
spirit, and its customs are more fully described, though here
as always in Björnson's work the people are primarily studied
as men and women, and secondarily as peasants and citizens;
and the descriptions are brief, incidental, and strictly subordinate to the story. We imagine in this an exercise of self-denial,
for Björnson must be in love with all that belongs to his char-

acters or surrounds them, to the degree of desiring to dwell longer than he ever does upon their portrayal. His fashion in dealing with scenery and character both is well shown in this account of Marit's party, to which Oeyvind was invited, and at which he ceases with his experience of the world to be the entirely happy boy of the past. . . .

The religious feeling which is a passive quality in "Arne" is a positive and controlling influence in "The Happy Boy," where it is chiefly exerted by the old schoolmaster. To him a long and bitter quarrel with an only brother, now dead, has taught lifelong meekness and dread of pride; and he affectingly rebukes Oeyvind's ambition to be first among the candidates for confirmation, in order that he may eclipse all others in Marit's eyes. But Björnson's religious feeling is not pietistic; on the contrary, it teaches, as in "The Fisher-Maiden," that a cheerful life of active goodness is the best interpretation of liberal and hopeful faith, and it becomes at no time a theological abstraction. It is always more or less blended with love of home, and a sense of the sweetness and beauty of natural affections. It is a strengthening property in the tenderness of a sentiment which seems almost distinctively his, or which at least is very clearly distinguished from German sentiment, and in which we Anglo-Saxon readers may indulge our hearts without that recoil of shame which otherwise attends the like surrender. Indeed, we feel a sort of inherent sympathy with most of Björnson's people on this and other accounts, as if we were in spirit, at least, Scandinavians with them, and the Viking blood had not yet died out of us. Some of the traits that he sketches are those now of New England fishermen and farmers and of Western pioneers,—that is, the pioneers of the time before Pacific Railroads. A conscientiousness also exists in them which is like our own,—for we have really a popular conscientiousness, in spite of many shocking appearances to the contrary,—though there seems to be practically more forgiveness in their morality than in ours, especially towards such errors as those by which Arne and Petra came to be. But their incentives and expectations are all as different from ours as their customs are, and in these romances the reader is always sensible of beholding the life of a vigorous and healthful yet innumerous people, restricted by an un-

friendly climate and variable seasons, and gaining a hard sub-
sistence from the treacherous sea and grudging soil. Sometimes the sense of nature's reluctant or cruel attitude toward
man finds open expression, as in "The Fisher-Maiden," where
the pastor says to the "village saints": "Your homes are far up
among the mountains, where your grain is cut down more frequently by the frost than by the scythe. Such barren fields and
deserted spots should never have been built upon; they might
well be given over to pasturage and the spooks. Spiritual life
thrives but poorly in your mountain-home, and partakes of the
gloom of the surrounding vegetation. Prejudice, like the cliffs
themselves, overhangs your life and casts a shadow upon it."
Commonly, however, the pathos of this unfriendliness between
the elements and man is not sharply uttered, but remains a
subtle presence qualifying all impressions of Norwegian life.
Perhaps it is this which gives their singular beauty to Björnson's pictures of the scenery amidst which the action of his
stories takes place,—pictures notably of Nature in her kindlier
moods, as if she were not otherwise to be endured by the
imagination.

In "The Fisher-Maiden," which is less perfect as a romance
than "Arne," Björnson has given us in Petra his most perfect
and surprising creation. The story is not so dreamy, and it has
not so much poetic intimacy with external things as "Arne,"
while it is less naturalistic than "The Happy Boy," and interests us in characters more independently of circumstance. It
is, however, very real, and Petra is a study as successful as
daring. . . . In a little space these people's characters are
shown in all their individual quaintness, their narrow life is
hinted in its gloom and loneliness, and the reader is made to
feel at once respect and compassion for them.

There is no room left here to quote from "The Fisher-
Maiden"; but the reader has already been given some idea of
Björnson's manner in the passages from "Arne" and "The
Happy Boy." This manner is always the same in its freedom
from what makes the manner of most of our own stories tedious and abominable: it is always direct, unaffected, and dignified, expressing nothing of the author's personality, while fully
interpreting his genius, and supplying no intellectual hollow-
ness and poverty with tricks and caprices of phrase.

We hope that his publishers will find it profitable to give us translations of all his works. From him we can learn that fulness exists in brevity rather more than in prolixity; that the finest poetry is not ashamed of the plainest fact; that the lives of men and women, if they be honestly studied, can, without surprising incident or advantageous circumstance, be made as interesting in literature as are the smallest private affairs of the men and women in one's own neighborhood; that telling a thing is enough, and explaining it too much; and that the first condition of pleasing is a generous faith in the reader's capacity to be pleased by natural and simple beauty.

Ivan Turgenev (1818—1883)

Between 1867, the date of the first English translation of
Fathers and Children, and 1873, the date of Howells' review of *Dimitri Roudine,* Turgenev was read, reviewed, and
discussed by such men as T. S. Perry, G. P. Lathrop, C. E.
Norton, Henry James—and William Dean Howells.

When Howells joined the staff of the *Atlantic Monthly* in
1866 he was still the literary youth from Ohio with a taste
for Thackeray and George Eliot. Besides a few poems in the
Atlantic and a sheaf of travel sketches sent home to the *Boston Daily Advertiser,* the young journalist had published nothing of literary importance. But in his editorial capacity he had
come to know Henry James, who, though six years his junior,
was ahead of Howells in his knowledge of the new way of
writing fiction; moreover, James knew the young men who
were discovering Turgenev. In a reminiscent article written
for the *North American Review* of July, 1912, Howells tells
us that Perry, to whom James had introduced him, first directed his attention to Russian literature and defined for him
Turgenev's contribution to realism.

By 1874, when James wrote an essay on Turgenev, Howells had reviewed a number of the Russian's novels in the *Atlantic.* As he tells in *My Literary Passions:* "In those years at
Cambridge my most notable literary experience without
doubt was the knowledge of Tourgenief's novels, which began
to be recognized in all their greatness about the middle of the
seventies." By sharing this "notable literary experience" with
readers of the *Atlantic,* Howells hoped, as he said in his review of *Smoke* in 1872, to introduce to the American public a worthier type of fiction. Again, in his review of *Dimitri
Roudine* he attempted to show the *Atlantic* readers "the kind
of novel which can alone keep the art of fiction from being
the weariness and derision of mature readers." More than ten
years before he consciously argued the cause of realism from
"The Editor's Study" of *Harper's Monthly,* Howells expressed
his disgust for the romantic pabulum dear to the nineteenth-

century fiction reader and his interest in the new realism reflected in Turgenev.

Howells' next review of Turgenev, in the *Atlantic* for February, 1873, showed that he was interested in *Liza* not only as a critic but also as a novelist. One can best explain the extraordinary gain in power that marked Howells' progress from *Suburban Sketches* (1871) through *Their Wedding Journey* (1872) to *A Chance Acquaintance* (1873) by a realization of Howells' debt to Turgenev. In this meditative review of *Liza* Howells remarked on Turgenev's objectivity, which he himself was attempting to achieve.

[He] never calls on you to admire how well he does a thing; he only makes you wonder at the truth and value of the thing when it is done. He seems the most self-forgetful of of the story-telling tribe, and he is no more enamoured of his creatures than of himself; he pets none of them; he upbraids none; you like them or hate them for what they are; it does not seem to be his affair.

When in later years Howells looked back at "one of the profoundest literary passions of my life," he still felt that Turgenev's "method is as far as art can go." What Howells meant by the art of Turgenev he defined very clearly in *My Literary Passions*:

His fiction is to the last degree dramatic. The persons are sparely described, and briefly accounted for, and then they are left to transact their affair, whatever it is, with the least possible comment or explanation from the author. The effect flows naturally from their characters, and when they have done or said a thing you conjecture why as unerringly as you would if they were people whom you knew outside of a book. I had already conceived of the possibility of this from Björnson, who practices the same method, but I was still too sunken in the gross darkness of English fiction to rise to full consciousness of its excellence. . . . It was with a joyful astonishment that I realized the great art of Tourgenief.

Though Howells' early biographer and critic, D. G. Cooke, thinks that traces of Dimitri Roudine are to be found in Don Ippolito in *A Foregone Conclusion*, it is not possible to define with exactness Howells' indebtedness to Turgenev. It is enough to say that Howells, at the very time when his critical creed and his technique as a novelist were being formed, had the good fortune to know intimately a group of young men who were eagerly learning the "lesson of the master"—objectivity tempered by a wide humanity. In an interview with Joyce Kilmer in 1914 Howells, then an old man, recalled that in those days on the *Atlantic* all the younger writers were reading Turgenev. This Russian writer, he remembered with appreciation, opened to him "a new world—and it was the only real world."

Greetings were exchanged between the two through Henry James, who had come to know the Russian novelist in Paris. Turgenev read and enjoyed Howells' novels and once remarked, "I have spent the night reading *A Chance Acquaintance*, and now I should like to visit a country where there are girls like the heroine." According to President Rutherford B. Hayes, Turgenev said that he enjoyed the writing of Howells more than that of "anyone now living." Abraham Cahan, a young writer and friend of Howells, recorded in his *Autobiography* the fact that Howells once showed him a letter he had received from Turgenev and remarked that he had met Turgenev in Paris.

A TURGENEV NOVEL*

Dimitri Roudine . . . is mainly the study of one man's character, but a character so complex that there is little to ask of the author in the way of a story. In fact Dimitri Roudine is

* *Dimitri Roudine*. A Novel. By Ivan Turgénieff, 1873. Appeared first in Russia in 1855. Translated and published in *Every Saturday* (January—June, 1873). This translation was made by T. S. Perry from French and German texts. Reviewed in the *Atlantic Monthly*, September, 1873.

himself sufficient plot; and the reader is occupied from the moment of his introduction with the skillful development of his various traits, to the exclusion of the other incidents and interests. The other persons of the fiction are of a kind which the reader of Turgénieff stories may begin to classify in some degree, or at least find in a certain measure familiar. The women are, as usual, very well portrayed, especially the young girl Natalie, whose ignorant trust, courage, love, and adoration for Roudine, changing to doubt and scorn,—whose whole maidenly being,—are expressed in a few scenes and phrases. Her mother, Daria Michaëlovna, is also exceedingly well done. She is of an entirely different type, a woman of mind, as she supposes, with advanced ideas, but really full of pride of caste, worldly, and slight of intellect, though not wanting in selfish shrewdness or a strong will. The reader ought to note with what delicacy, and yet with what force, Turgénieff indicates, in Alexandra Paulovna, a sweet, placid, self-contained maturity, alike different from the wild fragrance of Natalie's young girlhood and the artificial perfume of Daria's well-preserved middle life; though he could hardly fail to do this, for nothing is more observable in Turgénieff than his success in characterizing the different epochs of womanhood. Volinzoff's conscious intellectual inferiority to Natalie, and his simple, manly love for her are nearly all there is of him; Pigasoff, who peculated in office when younger and who in provincial retirement is a brutal censor of the follies of human nature, is rather a study than an actor in the drama which develops Roudine; and Leschnieff, who promises something in himself, and does really prove of firm and generous stuff, is after all hardly more than a relief and explanation of the principal person. It is he who expresses the first doubt of Roudine after that philosopher has made his appearance at Daria Michaëlovna's, crushing Pigasoff, bewildering and charming Natalie, mystifying Alexandra, and provoking Volinzoff. Leschnieff knew him in his student days, when filial love, friendship and all real things were lost in his habit of eloquent phrasing; when Roudine was cruelly ungrateful and mean in fact, that he might be magnanimous in the abstract; and the shadow of this dark recollection Leschnieff casts upon Roudine's new friends. He does not wish him to marry Natalie, who, he sees, is fascinated with him; but after Roudine's miserable weakness ends their love and all the others despise him, then Leschnieff does justice to his elevation of ideas and purposes. "He may have genius; I won't deny it; but the trouble is he has no character. . . . He is full of enthusiasm; and you can believe a phlegmatic man like me when I say that it is a most precious quality, especially in a time like the present. We are unendurably cold-blooded, indifferent, and apathetic. . . . Once when I was talking of Roudine I accused him of coldness. I was both just and unjust. His coldness is in his blood,—he's not to blame for it,—not in his head. I was wrong in calling him an actor; he is no swindler, no cheat; he does not live on other people like a parasite, but like a child. Yes, he may die in loneliness and misery, but shall we throw stones at him on that account? He will never accomplish anything because he lacks energy and a strong will; but who can say that he has never done, or never will do, any good? That his words have never sown good seed in some young heart, to which nature has not denied the force to carry out what it has conceived?"

It is touchingly related in an epilogue how, after several years, Roudine and Leschnieff came together by chance in the same inn. Leschnieff asks his old comrade to dine with him, and the two elderly men thee and thou each other in the student fashion. Roudine tells of his successive failures since they last met:

" 'Yes, brother,' he began, 'I can now cry with Kolzoff, "Where hast thou brought me, my youth? I have no longer where to lay my head!" . . . And was I really good for nothing, and was there nothing for me to do in this world? I have often asked myself this question, and, in spite of all my attempts to set myself lower in my own esteem, I can't help feeling that I have certain abilities which don't fall to the lot of every one. Why must this force remain powerless? Then, too, dost thou remember when we travelled abroad together, how self-confident and blind I was? . . . It is true, I didn't know definitely what I wanted, I revelled in the sound of my own voice, I chased vain phantoms. But now, on the contrary, I can say aloud to the whole world what it is I want; I have nothing to hide; I am, in the fullest sense of the word, a well-meaning man; I have become humble, I am willing to adapt myself to circumstances, I have limited my wishes, I don't strive for any remote object, I confine myself to doing even the slightest service; and yet I do not succeed in anything. What is the reason of this persistent failure? Why can't I live and work like others? I no sooner get a definite position, I no sooner establish myself somewhere, than fate casts me pitilessly out again. . . . I begin to fear my fate. . . . Why is this? Explain this puzzle!'

" 'Puzzle!' repeated Leschnieff. 'It is true, thou has always been a puzzle to me. Even in your youth, when I saw thee acting ill and speaking well in turn, and that time after time, even then I could not understand thee clearly; that was the reason I ceased to love thee. . . . Thou hast so much fire, so earnest a longing for the ideal.' . . .

" 'Words, nothing but words. Where are the deeds?' interrupted Roudine.

" 'Yes; but a good word is a deed too!'

"Roudine looked at Leschnieff without speaking, and shook his head."

We almost forget, in following this tender yet keen analysis of a pathetic character, that there is really something of a story in the book. Roudine imagines that he loves Natalie, and he wins her brave, inexperienced heart; but when their love is prematurely discovered to her mother, and Natalie comes to him ready to fly with him, to be his at any cost, he is paralyzed at the thought of Daria's opposition. "We must submit," he says. The scene that follows, with Natalie's amazement, wounded faith, and rising contempt and Roudine's shame and anguish, is terrible,—the one intensely dramatic passage in the book, and a masterpiece of literary art which we commend to all students and lovers of that art.

We are not quite sure whether we like or dislike the carefulness with which Roudine's whole character is kept from us, so that we pass from admiration to despite before we come finally to half-respectful compassion; and yet is this not the way it would be in life? Perhaps, also, if we fully understood him at first, his relations to the others would not so much interest us. But do we wholly understand him at last? This may be doubted, though in the mean time we are taught a merciful distrust of our own judgments, and we take Leschnieff's for-

giving and remorseful attitude towards him. It may be safely
surmised that this was the chief effect that Turgénieff desired
to produce in us; certainly he treats the story involved in the
portrayal of Roudine's character with almost contemptuous
indifference, letting three epilogues limp in after the first ram-
bling narrative has spent itself, and seeming to care for these
only as they further reveal the hero's traits. But for all this
looseness of construction, it is a very great novel,—as much
greater than the novel of incident as Hamlet is greater than
Richard III. It is of the kind of novel which can alone keep
the art of fiction from being the weariness and derision of
mature readers; and if it is most deeply melancholy, it is also
as lenient and thoughtful as a just man's experience of men.

Giovanni Verga (1840—1922)

Howells, during four years as consul in Venice, learned to love the daily sights and smells of the old city. One is not surprised, then, to find a paragraph of "The Editor's Study" for November, 1886, devoted to Verga's novel *I Malavoglia,* which Howells read first in Italian and introduced at once to his American readers. Howells recounts the story, "simply the history of a poor family trying to pay off an unjust debt and patiently suffering and even perishing in the long struggle." He then enlarges upon the misery of these fisherfolk of Sicily—the father lost at sea, a son killed in battle, another turning to crime, the mother dying of cholera. Such are "the incidents of this simple and beautiful story of these common people whom vulgar people call commonplace. It has an incomparable grasp of Italian actualities, as they present themselves on such a small stage—social, political, domestic and religious." The book, Howells adds, "is eminently worthy of translation."

The novel was, in fact, translated four years later by Mary A. Craig with the title *The House by the Medlar-Tree.* Howells quite appropriately wrote the introduction, which is printed below. Until a new translation was made by Eric Mosbacher in 1953, this nineteenth-century version remained the only one available in English. The critic who reviewed the current translation in *The New York Times Book Review* glanced briefly back at Howells and expressed surprise that Howells, with "his usual flair and competence," wrote for his introduction "that rare thing—a sincere panegyric." What Howells said about *The House by the Medlar-Tree* was, to his readers of 1890, more than "a sincere panegyric": his review was an episode in the critical discussion of realism or—to use Verga's term—*veritism.* The novel was another vindication of Howells' insistence that, without describing extraordinary people engaged in romantic adventure, without departing from the simple truth of the daily lives of simple people, one can hear the sad poetry of ordinary existence. Moreover, the "lesson" of the story is that of life everywhere, that goodness

47

brings not pleasure but peace to the soul. This inescapable conclusion is expressed by Verga in the circumstances of his tale rather than in the comments of the author. For he, like Turgenev, is an impassive observer of his little drama and achieves his effects by means of a subtle reticence.

Howells, in his quarrel with the "great mass" of readers who prefer "to read the Rider Haggards and the Rudyard Kiplings of the day," points to Verga as an example of the "new spirit" on the Continent. Howells recognized at once that Kipling had "a future," but observed that "there is little in the knowingness and swagger of his performance that is not to be deplored with many tears; it is really so far away from the thing that ought to be." However, the reader need not look to the English for light on fiction. "We must turn to the more artistic people for it, to the Continental writers whose superiority in fiction has often been celebrated here." Howells invites the reader to take *The House by the Medlar-Tree* and "examine a little its structure and material." Here nothing is "operated and explained"; "the characters and conditions" are "frankly left to find their own way to the reader's appreciation" of their universal truth.

Though Howells did not meet or correspond with Verga, whose life span very nearly corresponded to his own, he did list the books of this "contemporary Italian" among his "passions" for reasons that the following introduction makes more clear to the reader of today than to the reader of the 1890's. "For my own part," wrote one subscriber to the *Atlantic* (May, 1892), after reading *The House by the Medlar-Tree*, "I think that a preface by Mr. Howells, recommending a book for its realism, will hereafter be enough to guard me against it. Some may agree with him to prize such novels as masterpieces of modern art, but is the depression they produce a wholesome effect to receive from a work of art?"

THE HOUSE BY THE MEDLAR-TREE*

Any one who loves simplicity or respects sincerity, any one who feels the tie binding us all together in the helplessness of

our common human life, and running from the lowliest as
well as the highest to Mystery immeasurably above the whole
earth, must find a rare and tender pleasure in this simple story
of an Italian fishing village. I cannot promise that it will interest any other sort of readers, but I do not believe that any
other sort are worth interesting; and so I can praise Signor
Verga's book without reserve as one of the most perfect
pieces of literature that I know.

When we talk of the great modern movement towards
reality we speak without the documents if we leave this book
out of the count, for I can think of no other novel in which
the facts have been more faithfully reproduced, or with a pro-
founder regard for the poetry that resides in facts and resides
nowhere else. Signor Verga began long ago, in his *Vita dei
Campi* ("Life of the Fields"), to give proof of his fitness to
live in our time; and after some excursions in the region of
French naturalism, he here returns to the original sources of
his inspiration, and offers us a masterpiece of the finest realism.

He is, I believe, a Sicilian, of that meridional race among
whom the Italian language first took form, and who in these
latest days have done some of the best things in Italian literature. It is of the far South that he writes, and of people whose
passions are elemental and whose natures are simple. The
characters, therefore, are types of good and of evil, of good
and of generosity, of truth and of falsehood. They are not the
less personal for this reason, and the life which they embody
is none the less veritable. It will be well for the reader who
comes to this book with the usual prejudices against the
Southern Italians to know that such souls as Padron 'Ntoni
and Maruzza La Longa, with their impassioned conceptions
of honor and duty, exist among them; and that such love
idyls as that of Mena and Alfio, so sweet, so pure, and the
happier but not less charming every-day romance of Alessio
and Nunziata, are passages of a life supposed wholly benighted
and degraded. This poet, as I must call the author, does
again the highest office of poetry, in making us intimate with

* Translated by Mary A. Craig, with Introduction by W. D.
Howells, 1890.

the hearts of men of another faith, race, and condition, and
teaching us how like ourselves they are in all that is truest in
them. Padron 'Ntoni and La Longa, Luca, Mena, Alfio,
Nunziata, Alessio, if harshlier named, might pass for New
England types, which we boast the product of Puritanism,
but which are really the product of conscience and order. The
children of disorder who move through the story—the selfish,
the vicious, the greedy, like Don Sylvestro, and La Vespa, and
Goosefoot, and Dumb-bell, or the merely weak, like poor
'Ntoni Malavoglia—are not so different from our own images
either, when seen in this clear glass, which falsifies and dis-
torts nothing.

Few tales, I think, are more moving, more full of heart-
break, than this; for few are so honest. By this I mean that
the effect in it is precisely that which the author aimed at. He
meant to let us see just what manner of men and women
went to make up the life of a little Italian town of the present
day, and he meant to let the people show themselves with the
least possible explanation or comment from him. The trans-
action of the story is in the highest degree dramatic; but
events follow one another with the even sequence of hours
on the clock. You are not prepared to value them before-
hand; they are not advertised to tempt your curiosity like
feats promised at the circus, in the fashion of the feebler novels; often it is in the retrospect that you recognize their importance and perceive their full significance. In this most
subtly artistic management of his material the author is most
a master, and almost more than any other he has the rare
gift of trusting the intelligence of his reader. He seems to
have no more sense of authority or supremacy concerning
the personages than any one of them would have in telling
the story, and he has as completely freed himself from liter-
osity as the most unlettered among them. Under his faithful
touch life seems mainly sad in Trezza, because life is mainly
sad everywhere, and because men there have not yet adjusted
themselves to the only terms which can render life tolerable
anywhere. They are still rivals, traitors, enemies, and have
not learned that in the vast orphanage of nature they have no
resource but love and union among themselves and submis-
sion to the unfathomable wisdom which was before they

were. Yet seen aright this picture of a little bit of the world, very common and low down and far off, has a consolation which no one need miss. There, as in every part of the world, and in the whole world, goodness brings not pleasure, not happiness, but it brings peace and rest to the soul, and lightens all burdens; the trial and the sorrow go on for good and evil alike; only, those who choose the evil have no peace.

Armando Palacio Valdés (1853—1938)

"This time I made the Study mainly about Tolstoy, Gogol, and Valdés," Howells wrote in January, 1886, to his old friend, Thomas Sergeant Perry, and added: "But isn't it strange that in all this vast land there should not be one intelligent voice besides yours on the right side?"

What Howells meant by "the right side" becomes clear as one reads the six reviews of the novels of Armando Palacio Valdés that he wrote for "The Editor's Study" between 1886 and 1891. The first and the last of this significant group are presented below.

But before turning to these reviews and the critical controversy on the meaning of realism to which they contribute, one must remember that Howells' love for Spanish literature began many years earlier when he was a child in Ohio. The elder Howells, his son tells us, used to recount the story of Don Quixote in the large family kitchen of the home in Hamilton, while "we boys were all shelling peas." The ten-year-old boy made such good use of a Spanish-English dictionary given to his father by a soldier of the Mexican War that he taught himself the rudiments of the Spanish language. One is not surprised to discover that he read the novels of Valdés in Spanish before they appeared in English translations and was therefore able to introduce them to American readers almost as soon as they were published abroad.

The first Valdés novel that Howells reviewed for the Study (April, 1886) and referred to in his letter to Perry was *Marta y Maria* (1883). Howells tells us in *My Literary Passions* that he read very little during his year abroad in 1882 and that it was not until he returned to Boston, "in the old atmosphere of work," that he turned again to books. Undertaking "a critical department in one of the magazines" made Howells feel again "the rise of the old enthusiasm for an author"—this time for two contemporary Spanish writers, Valera and Valdés. The latter, hitherto unknown to Howells, delighted him "beyond words by his friendly and abundant

52

humor, his feeling for character and his subtle insight." Howells was so impressed by the story of two sisters, Marta and Maria, who fell in love with the same man, that he called the novel "one of the most truthful and profound I have ever read." Did the story of the rivalry of the two sisters linger in Howells' mind when he wrote of a similar situation in *The Rise of Silas Lapham* two years later? Since his interest in a novel was always that of both novelist and critic, we are tempted to wonder whether he read Valdés' new novel when it appeared in 1883, and whether in Valdés' story he found a hint for his own.

"Of course it is a realistic novel," said Howells in his review of *Marta y Maria*, and he added, "It is even by an author who has written essays upon realism." One of these essays, the Prologue to *Marta y Maria*, was so good, he assured his readers, that he would have been glad to reprint it in full. In it Valdés said:

> I have the presumption to believe that, though *Marta y Maria* may not be beautiful, it is a realistic novel. I know that realism—at the present time called naturalism—has many impulsive adepts, who conceive that truth exists only in the vulgar incidents of life, and that these are the only ones worth transferring to art. Fortunately this is not the case. Outside of markets, garrets, and slums, the truth exists no less. The very apostle of naturalism, Émile Zola, confesses this by painting scenes of polished and lofty poetry which assuredly conflict with his exaggerated aesthetic theories.

Valdés was frequently referred to by Howells in "The Editor's Study" during this decade, not only because he enjoyed the natural, direct, humorous, and often poetic novels of the Spaniard, but also because Valdés, within his own limits, reinforced Howells' ideas of realism. In the November, 1886, issue of *Harper's*, Howells announced that *Marta y Maria* could now be read in translation, and he reviewed briefly the next two novels of Valdés, *José* (1885) and *Riverita* (1886), *Maxima* (1888), *El Cuarto poder* (1888), and *Scum* (1891), Howells commented on in turn as they appeared.

Howells was in fact so impressed by *Scum* that he discussed it in "The Editor's Study" for February and again for April, 1891. It is the second of these two reviews that is printed below, because it reflects Howells' enlarged sense of the social scope of the novel. In the Study for February he remarked that *Scum*

> . . . recognizes, once for all, that it is the top of aristocratic and plutocratic "society" in all countries which is really the scum, and not those poor plebeian dregs which mostly boil about the bottom of the caldron and never get to the surface at all. . . . The book is important because it is a part of that expression of contemporary thought about contemporary things now informing fiction in all countries but England.

Valdés was, according to Howells, one of the few writers who knew that all of life is the province of the novelist; that it belongs to no class; that the realistic novelist reflects the truth that resides in the simple life about him and disdains the tricks of plot and melodrama, called by Valdés "effectism"; that in holding to this program he produces a work of art full of the joy of life, not weighted down with sordidness and sorrow.

In agreeing with Howells that Valdés' novel is a contribution to realism, Perry puts himself on the "right side" of the controversy raging, with varying emphasis, in most of the countries of Europe more violently than in the United States. "You're right," says Howells to Perry in the letter quoted above, "no one invented realism; it came. It's perfectly astonishing that it seems to have come everywhere at once."

Howells' hope was that realism would come to this country too, especially in the form represented by the three contemporary Spanish novelists to whom he frequently referred, Galdós, Pardo-Bazán, and Valdés. Of the three, Valdés is the one with whom Howells was the most familiar, and in fact the only one with whom he had personal relations. In a note placed before a letter to Howells from Valdés, Mildred Howells wrote, "Howells greatly admired the work of Valdés and they often wrote to each other, Valdés in Spanish and Howells in Italian." In this letter of November 26, 1887, Valdés expressed his appreciation of the reviews of his novels appearing in *Harper's* and observed, "I believe that a mysterious current of sympathy joins our hearts and minds across the ocean—the same things impress or disgust us." Affectionate letters were exchanged between the two novelist-critics, and their books were sent back and forth across the Atlantic. "I am reading a new book by Valdés, perfectly charming," wrote Howells to Perry in July, 1911. Howells was then seventy-four, but still charmed by the Spanish novelist.

Though Howells felt that he must occasionally warn "the intending reader" of the "Latin frankness" to be found in a novel by Valdés, and though he felt more than once that "Valdés helps himself out with a romantic and superfluous bit of self-sacrifice," Howells thoroughly enjoyed the good sense, the sweetness, and the humor of the Spaniard's tales. "This delightful author" further pleased Howells by the essay on fiction with which he prefaced one of his novels, the charming story of *Sister Saint Sulpice:* "It is an essay which I wish every one intending to read, or even to write a novel, might acquaint himself with." So well, indeed, did Howells acquaint himself with this Prologue, which appeared in 1889, that his comments on Valdés' critical views fill Sections XIII—XIV of *Criticism and Fiction*.

MARTA Y MARIA*

One would not perhaps look first to find [examples of the best in fiction] in Spain, but we have just been reading a Spanish novel which is very nearly one. Of course it is a realistic novel; it is even by an author who has written essays upon realism, and who feels obliged, poor fellow, in choosing a theme which deals with the inside rather than the outside of life, to protest that the truth exists within us as well as without, and is not confined to the market-houses, the dram-shops, the street corners, or the vulgar facts of existence. Don Ar-

---

* *Marta y Maria,* by Armando Palacio Valdés, 1883. Reviewed in *Harper's Monthly*, April, 1886.

mando Palacio Valdés believes that his *Marta y Maria* is a
realistic novel, although it is not founded upon current and
common events, and that the beautiful and the noble also lie
within the realm of reality. We should ourselves go a little farther, and say that they are to be found nowhere else; but we
have not at present to do with our opinions, or even the prologue to Senor Valdés's novel, though we should be glad to reproduce that in full, it is so good. We must speak, however,
of the admirable little illustrations of his book, so full of
character and spirit and movement. They are badly printed,
and the cover of the book, stamped in black and silver, is as
ugly as a "burial casket," but our censure must almost wholly
end with the mechanical execution of the book. The literature
is delightful: full of charming humor, tender pathos, the liveli-
est sympathy with nature, the keenest knowledge of human
nature, and a style whose charm makes itself felt through the
shadows of a strange speech. It is the story of two sisters,
daughters of the chief family in a Spanish sea-port city: Maria, who passes from the romance of literature to the romance
of religion, and abandons home, father, and lover to become
the spouse of heaven, and Marta, who remains to console all
these for her loss. We do not remember a character more finely studied than that of Maria, who is followed, not satirically
or ironically, through all the involutions of a conscious, artificial personality, but with masterly divination, and is shown
as essentially cold-hearted and selfish in her religious abnegation, and as sensuous in her spiritual ecstasies as she was in
her abandon to the romances on which she fed her egoistic
fancy. But Marta—Marta is delicious! We see her first as an
awkward girl of thirteen at her mother's *tertulia,* helplessly
laughing at some couples who give a few supererogatory
hops in the dance after the music suddenly stops; and the note
of friendly simplicity, of joyous, frank, sweet naturalness,
struck in the beginning, is felt in her character throughout.
Nothing could be lovelier than the portrayal of this girl's affection for her father and mother, and of the tenderness that in-
sensibly grows up between her and her sister's lover, left step
by step in the lurch by the intending bride of heaven. One of
the uses of realism is to make us know people; to make us understand that the Spaniards, for example, are not the remote

cloak-and-sword gentry of opera which romance has painted them, abounding in guitars, poniards, billets, *autos-da-fe,* and confessionals, but are as "like folks" as we are. It seems that there is much of that freedom among young people with them which makes youth a heavenly holiday in these favored States. Maria's lover has "the run of the house," in this Spanish town, quite as he would have in Chicago or Portland, and he follows Marta about in the frequent intervals of Maria's neglect; he makes her give him lunch in the kitchen when he is hungry, this very human young Marquis de Penalta; he helps her to make a pie, the young lady having a passion for all domestic employments, and to put away the clean clothes. Her father, Don Mariano Elorza, has a passion for the smell of freshly ironed linen, much as any well-domesticated American citizen might have, and loves to go and put his nose in the closets where it hangs. His wife has been a tedious, complaining invalid all her married life, but he is heart-broken when she dies; and it is at this moment that Maria—who has compromised him in the Carlist movement because that is the party of the Church, and has tried in the same cause to make her lover turn traitor to the government which he has sworn as citizen and soldier to defend—comes ecstatic from the death-scene to ask his permission to complete her vocation in the convent. He gives it with a sort of disdain for her pitiless and senseless egotism. The story closes with the happy love of Marta and Ricardo, clasped to the old man's breast and mingling their tears with his; and the author cries, "O eternal God, who dwellest in the hearts of the good, can it be that these tears are less grateful to Thee than the mystical colloquies of the Convent of St. Bernard?"

A sketch of the story gives no idea of its situations, or, what is more difficult and important, the atmosphere of reality in which it moves. The whole social life of the quiet town is skillfully suggested, and an abundance of figures pass before us, all graphically drawn, none touched with weakness or exaggeration. It is a book with a sole blemish—a few pages in which the author thinks it necessary to paint the growth of little Marta's passion in too vivid colors. There is no great harm; but it is a lapse of taste and of art that libels a lovely character, and seems a sacrifice to the ugly French fetich which has possessed itself of the good name of Realism to befoul it.

SCUM*

The whole essay [*The Palpitating Question,* by Emilia Pardo-Bazán] is redolent of the Spanish humor, which is so like our own, and yet has its peculiar perfume. This humor is what forms the atmosphere of Valdés's novels, and keeps his satire kindly even when his contempt is strongest, as in that last novel of his, which his translator calls *Scum,* and which deals with society as Valdés "found it" in Madrid. Certain points of resemblance are to be found in "good" society the world over, nowadays, and one of these is its decorous religiosity. It appears that wherever people so far experience the favor of Heaven as to have nothing to do but to dress handsomely and to fare sumptuously, they are as punctilious in their devotions as they are in any of their social duties. Nothing could be more edifying than the Spanish novelist's study of the "smart set" of Madrid as he pictures them at a select service in the oratory of a devout lady of their number. They seem certainly to be more vicious than any smart set among ourselves, or at least differently vicious, but they vary little in their theory of life. If they worship God they do not forget their duty to Mammon, and money is to the fore among them as it is among us. One of their leaders is Clementina, the heroine, if the book can be said to have a heroine, who is the daughter of the Duke of Raquena, a robber baron of the stock exchange, an adventurer in Cuba, ennobled for his unscrupulous rapacity in accumulating money, after he returns to Spain. He is a great financier, as such people are with us, sometimes; he knows how to get up "corners" and to "squeeze" those he traps into them, quite as if he were an oil or wheat operator. He is the owner of some great quicksilver mines, and one of the most striking passages of the book is the account of the visit he pays these mines with a party of the

---

* *Scum,* by Armando Palacio Valdés, 1890. Reviewed in *Harper's Monthly,* April, 1891.

"best" people of Madrid in his train of private cars. They are all hanging upon him in the hope that he will somehow make them rich, but some of the women are shocked at the life, or the death in life, of the miners, who are sufferers from mercurial poisoning, and who go shaking about like decrepit paralytics. The duke tells the ladies that the notion of mercurial poisoning is nonsense, and if the men would leave off drinking they would be well enough; just as one of our own millionaires has told us that the great cause of poverty is "intemperance." The duke's assurance comforts the ladies, and they have a banquet in one of the upper levels of the mine, while all round and under them the haggard miners are digging their own graves. Their gayety is a little chilled by the ironies of the young physician of the company, who takes a less optimistic view of the case than the good duke, though his life is spent among the miners and devoted to them. This physician is a socialist; and it is a curious sign of the times that the socialists should be making their way, in fiction at least, as the friends rather than the enemies of the race.

Benito Pérez Galdós (1845—1920)

"There is probably no chair of literature in this country . . .
which teaches young men anything of the universal impulse
which has given us the books not only of Zola, but of Tour-
guéneff and Tolstoi in Russia, of Björnsen in Norway, of
Valera in Spain, of Verga in Italy," Howells complained in
"The Editor's Study" of February, 1886. Five years later in
Criticism and Fiction he added the names of Ibsen, Valdés,
and Galdós, for he was always adding to his acquaintance of
foreign writers. Before he entered the Study in January,
1886, he had refused professorships at four institutions,
Union College and Washington University in 1868, Johns
Hopkins University in 1882, and Harvard University in
1886. When later a similar invitation came from Yale,
Howells again refused, for he did not consider himself a teacher; he preferred to educate his generation in European fiction
through the columns of *Harper's Magazine*.

Introducing the Spanish novelist Benito Pérez Galdós to the
American reader in *Harper's*, May, 1888, Howells compared his recently translated romance, *La familia de Leon
Roch*, to Valdés' *Marta y Maria;* "In *Leon Roch*, as in *Marta
y Maria*, the name of the devotee is Maria, but in this case she
is not an exalted sentimentalist seeking the fulfillment of her
selfish pietistic dreams in a convent, but a loving wife whom
her religious intolerance transforms into a monster of cruelty
and folly." Howells thus presented *Leon Roch* to the reader
as an example of the bigotry of the Roman Catholic Church;
in the opening paragraph, however, he pointed out that "we
cannot hug ourselves upon the freedom of the Protestant faith
from such forms of bigotry: it is the touch of poor human nature in [the] heroines [of Galdós and Valdés] which makes
them universally recognizable as portraits from life," according to Howells, and is far more important in a novel than the
social issues involved. Though Maria "is the terrible spirit of
bigotry," nevertheless, she and all her family "are really a
delightful group, with their several vices." In fact, it is "hard

not to give one's heart" to people "drawn with such wonderful truth," scoundrels though they be. But none of the individuals in this novel by Galdós is entirely good or evil; they belong, rather, to "those mixed characters who are beginning to get out of life into fiction. . . . No other sort seems to get into Galdós's book, and perhaps this is the reason why some of his most reprobate people have a hold upon our sympathies" and leave us finally with a sense of personal acquaintance.

These excerpts from the first of the two reviews Howells wrote of Galdós' novels indicate that he perceived at once the critical problem latent in *Leon Roch*, that of relating a social issue to the story of character in such a way as to allow the individual to dominate the background. Galdós, a Spanish liberal, interested in the social conditions of authoritarian Spain of the nineteenth century, recognized the novelist's difficulty early in his writing career. He, like Howells, objected to the historical romance, popular in the 1860's, and determined to concentrate as a novelist, first on social questions and later on the character of the individual, to which he subordinated social conditions. *La Fontana de Ora* (1867-1868) is essentially a historical novel; *Elandez* (1871) is social in intent: *Doña Perfecta* (1876) is the most dramatic example of Galdós' successful presentation of a character caught in a mesh of environmental factors. It is this greatest of all Galdós' novels that was the subject of Howells' second review. Though *Doña Perfecta* appeared two years before *La familia de Leon Roch*, it was not translated until 1895. The introduction to the translation by Mary E. Serrano was written by Howells; it had already appeared in *Harper's Bazar* on November 2, 1895, one week before the publication of the book, and this is the text printed below.

"The very acute and lively Spanish critic who signs himself Clarín," to whom Howells referred in the opening paragraph of his essay, was Leopoldo Alas (1852-1901), a brilliant professor from Oviedo, himself a novelist, critic, and editor, widely read—and feared—in Spain. He was a friend of the three Spanish authors most frequently referred to by Howells, Palacio Valdés, Pardo-Bazán, and Peréz Galdós; his admiration for Galdós dated back to student days, when he predicted that Galdós would regenerate the novel in Spain. Clarín hailed *Doña Perfecta* for its frank presentation of the truth about the provincial little town of Orbajosa, which he considered a microcosm of reactionary Spain.

Howells reflected Clarín's ideas in his review; one suspects that many more of Howells' critical concepts are to be found in the articles Clarín wrote for *El Solfeo*, a liberal journal of Madrid, from 1875 to the end of the century. The Spanish critic, like Howells, was convinced of the beauty as well as the truth of Galdós' novel, *Doña Perfecta*, which he reviewed in *El Solfeo*, October 20, 1876. He conceived of literature as one of the chief instruments of cultural improvement; the novelist might influence social evolution if he put "art" before "reform," and if he followed the road of realism rather than that of naturalism, which is merely photographic, or of romanticism, which is unrelated to actuality. "The method of the modern novel," then, is not that of naturalism, which readily becomes "tendencious" by overstressing the social issues, nor is it that of romanticism, which aspires to idealism. It is the method of the "new realism," which presents a psychological study of character in its environment.

Howells found similar critical ideas discussed in *La Cuestion Palpitante*, by Emilia Pardo-Bazán, the third of the trio admired by Clarín and Howells; she was, Howells tells us, a "valiant lady in the campaign for realism," who wrote "one of the best and strongest books on the subject" of the "new realism." This long essay Howells read in Spanish before he published *Criticism and Fiction*. These are the three Spanish writers whom Howells names in *My Literary Passions*, published the same year as the review below. These are the three whom Howells thought of when, in May, 1899, he commented in a rueful mood on the Spanish-American War, which had just ended: "If by any effect of advancing civility," he wrote, "we could have treated with Spain for the cession of her three novelists, Pérez Galdós, Emilia Pardo-Bazán, and Armando Palacio Valdés, I, for one American, should have been more content than I am with Cuba, Puerto Rico, and the Philippines." For it was with these three that Howells shared his distaste for the historical novel and his faith in the "new realism."

DONA PERFECTA, A GREAT NOVEL*

The very acute and lively Spanish critic who signs himself Clarín, and is known personally as Don Leopoldo Alas, says the present Spanish novel has no yesterday, but only a day-before-yesterday. It does not derive from the romantic novel which immediately preceded it, but it derives from the realistic novel which preceded that; the novel, large or little, as it was with Cervantes, Hurtado de Mendoza, Quevedo, and the masters of picaresque fiction.

Clarín dates its renascence from the political revolution of 1868, which gave Spanish literature the freedom necessary to the fiction that studies to reflect modern life, actual ideas, and current aspirations; and though its authors were few at first, "they have never been adventurous spirits, friends of Utopia, revolutionists, or impatient progressists and reformers." He thinks that the most daring, the most advanced, of the new Spanish novelists, and the best by far, is Don Pérez Galdós.

I should myself have made my little exception in favor of Don Armando Palacio Valdés, but Clarin speaks with infinitely more authority, and I am certainly ready to submit when he goes on to say that Galdós is not a social or literary insurgent; that he has no political or religious prejudices; that he shuns extremes, and is charmed with prudence; that his novels do not attack the Catholic dogmas—though they deal so severely with Catholic bigotry—but the customs and ideas cherished by secular fanaticism to the injury of the Church. because this is so evident, our critic holds, his novels are "found in the bosom of families in every corner of Spain." Their popularity among all classes in Catholic and prejudiced Spain, and not among free-thinking students merely, bears testimony to the fact that his aim and motive are understood

---

* *Doña Perfecta*, by B. Pérez Galdós. Reviewed in *Harper's Bazar*, November 2, 1895.

and appreciated, although his stories are apparently so often anti-Catholic.

Doña Perfecta is, first of all, a story, and a great story, but it is certainly also a story that must appear at times potently, and even bitterly, anti-Catholic. Yet it would be a pity and an error to read it with the preoccupation that it was an anti-Catholic tract, for really it is not that. If the persons were changed in name and place, and modified in passion to fit a cooler air, it might equally seem an anti-Presbyterian or anti-Baptist tract; for what it shows in the light of their own hatefulness and cruelty are the perversions of any religion, any creed. It is not, however, a tract at all; it deals in artistic largeness with the passion of bigotry, as it deals with the passion of love, the passion of ambition, the passion of revenge. But Galdós is Spanish and Catholic, and for him bigotry wears a Spanish and Catholic face. That is all.

Up to a certain time, I believe, Galdós wrote romantic or idealistic novels, and one of these I have read, and it tired me very much. It was called *Marianela,* and it surprised me the more because I was already acquainted with his later work, which is all realistic. But one does not turn realist in a single night, and although the change in Galdós was rapid, it was not quite a lightning change; perhaps because it was not merely an outward change, but artistically a change of heart. His acceptance in his quality of realist was much more instant than his conversion, and vastly wider; for we are told by the critic whom I have been quoting that Galdós's earlier efforts, which he called *Episodios Nacionales,* never had the vogue which his realistic novels have enjoyed.

These were, indeed, tendencious, if I may anglicize a very necessary word from the Spanish *tendencioso.* That is, they dealt with very obvious problems, and had very distinct and poignant significations, at least in the case of Doña Perfecta, Leon Roch, and Gloria. In still later novels, Emilia Pardo-Bazán thinks, he has comprehended that "the novel of to-day must take note of the ambient truth, and realize the beautiful with freedom and independence." This valiant lady, in the campaign for realism which she made under the title of *La Cuestión Palpitante*—one of the best and strongest books on the subject—counts him first among Spanish realists as Clarín counts him first among Spanish novelists. "With a certain fundamental humanity," she says, "a certain magisterial simplicity in his creations, with the natural tendency of his clear intelligence toward the truth, and with the frankness of his observation, the great novelist was always disposed to pass over to realism with arms and munitions; but his aesthetic inclinations were idealistic, and only in his latest works has he adopted the method of the modern novel, fathomed more and more the human heart, and broken once for all with the picturesque and with the typical personages, to embrace the earth we tread."

For her, as I confess for me, *Doña Perfecta* is not realistic enough—realistic as it is; for realism at its best is not tendencious. It does not seek to grapple with human problems, but is richly content with portraying human experiences; and I think Señora Pardo-Bazán is right in regarding Dona Perfecta as transitional, and of a period when the author had not yet assimilated in its fullest meaning the faith he had imbibed.

Yet it is a great novel, as I said; and perhaps because it is transitional it will please the greater number who never really arrive anywhere, and who like to find themselves in good company *en route*. It is so far like life that it is full of significations which pass beyond the persons and actions involved, and envelop the reader, as if he too were a character of the book, or rather as if its persons were men and women of this thinking, feeling, and breathing world, and he must recognize their experiences as veritable facts. From the first moment to the last it is like some passage of actual events in which you cannot withhold your compassion, your abhorrence, your admiration, any more than if they took place within your personal knowledge. Where they transcend all facts of your personal knowledge, you do not accuse them of improbability, for you feel them potentially in yourself, and easily account for them in the alien circumstance. I am not saying that the story has no faults; it has several. There are tags of romanticism fluttering about it here and there; and at times the author permits himself certain old-fashioned literary airs and poses and artifices, which you simply wonder at. It is in spite of these, and with all these defects, that it is so great and beautiful a book.

What seems to be so very admirable in the management of

the story is the author's success in keeping his own counsel. This may seem a very easy thing; but, if the reader will think over the novelists of his acquaintance, he will find that it is at least very uncommon. They mostly give themselves away almost from the beginning, either by their anxiety to hide what is coming, or their vanity in hinting what great things they have in store for the reader. Galdós does neither the one nor the other. He makes it his business to tell the story as it grows; to let the characters unfold themselves in speech and action; to permit the events to happen unheralded. He does not prophesy their course; he does not forecast the weather even for twenty-four hours; the atmosphere becomes slowly, slowly, but with occasional lifts and reliefs, of such a brooding breathlessness, of such a deepening density, that you feel the wild passion-storm nearer and nearer at hand, till it bursts at last; and then you are astonished that you had not foreseen it yourself from the first moment.

Next to this excellent method which I count the supreme characteristic of the book merely because it represents the whole, and the other facts are in the nature of parts, is the masterly conception of the characters. They are each typical of a certain side of human nature, as most of our personal friends and enemies are; but not exclusively of this side or that. They are each of mixed motives, mixed qualities; none of them is quite a monster; though those who are badly mixed do such monstrous things.

Pepe Rey, who is such a good fellow—so kind, and brave, and upright, and generous, so fine a mind, and so high a soul—is tactless and imprudent; he even condescends to the thought of intrigue; and though he rejects his plots at last, his nature has once harbored deceit. Don Inocencio, the priest, whose control of Doña Perfecta's conscience has vitiated the very springs of goodness in her, is by no means bad, aside from his purposes. He loves his sister and her son tenderly, and wishes to provide for them by the marriage which Pepe's presence threatens to prevent. The nephew, though selfish and little, has moments of almost being a good fellow; the sister, though she is really such a lamb of meekness, becomes a cat, and scratches Don Inocencio dreadfully when he weakens in his design against Pepe.

Rosario, one of the sweetest and purest images of girlhood that I know in fiction, abandons herself with equal passion to the love she feels for her cousin Pepe, and to the love she feels for her mother, Doña Perfecta. She is ready to fly with him, and yet she betrays him to her mother's pitiless hate.

But it is Doña Perfecta herself who is the transcendent figure, the most powerful creation of the book. In her, bigotry and its fellow-vice, hypocrisy, have done their perfect work, until she comes near to being a devil and really does a devil's deeds. Yet even she is not without some extenuating traits. Her bigotry springs from her conscience, and she is truly devoted to her daughter's eternal welfare; she is of such a native frankness that at a certain point she tears aside her mask of dissimulation and lets Pepe see all the ugliness of her perverted soul. She is wonderfully managed. At what moment does she begin to hate him, and to wish to undo her own work in making a match between him and her daughter? I could defy any one to say. All one knows is that at one moment she adores her brother's son, and at another she abhors him, and has already subtly entered upon her efforts to thwart the affection she has invited in him for her daughter.

Caballuco, what shall I say of Caballuco? He seems altogether bad, but the author lets one imagine that this cruel, this ruthless brute must have somewhere about him traits of lovableness, of leniency, though he never lets one see them. His gratitude to Doña Perfecta, even his murderous devotion, is not altogether bad; and he is certainly worse than nature made him, when wrought upon by her fury and the suggestion of Don Inocencio. The scene where they work him up to rebellion and assassination is a compendium of the history of intolerance; as the mean little conceited city of Orbajosa is the microcosm of bigoted and reactionary Spain.

I have called, or half-called, this book tendencious; but in a certain larger view it is not so. It is the eternal interest of passion working upon passion, not the temporary interest of condition antagonizing condition, which renders Doña Perfecta so poignantly interesting, and which makes its tragedy immense. But there is hope as well as despair in such a tragedy. There is the strange support of a bereavement in it, the consolation of feeling that for those who have suffered unto death, nothing can harm them more; that even for those who have inflicted their suffering this peace will soon come.

"Is Pérez Galdós a pessimist?" asks the critic Clarín. "No, certainly; but if he is not, why does he paint us sorrows that seem inconsolable? Is it from love of paradox? Is it to show that his genius, which can do so much, can paint the shadow lovelier than the light? Nothing of this. Nothing that is not serious, honest, and noble is to be found in this novelist. Are they pessimistic, those ballads of the North, that always end with vague resonances of woe? Are they pessimists, those singers of our own land, who surprise us with tears in the midst of laughter? Is Nature pessimistic, who is so sad at nightfall that it seems as if day were dying forever? The sadness of art, like that of nature, is a form of hope. Why is Christianity so artistic? Because it is the religion of sadness."

Henrik Ibsen (1828—1906)

When in 1895 Howells considered his tastes as a reader, he did not see fit to devote a chapter of *My Literary Passions* to Ibsen. Instead he referred to "the cold fascination" of the Norwegian, in contrast to the "delight" of Björnson, who held for him nothing of Ibsen's "scornful despair, nothing of his anarchistic contempt." However, Howells added, "I should be far from denying [Ibsen's] mighty mastery."

In spite of Howells' lack of temperamental sympathy for Ibsen, he frequently listed him, next to Zola and Tolstoy, among the Continental writers as a chief ally in the defense of realism. Why, he demanded in *Criticism and Fiction,* have not the critics in this country felt this "universal impulse"? In "The Editor's Easy Chair" of May, 1911, he repeated the list of those the Study had "preached" in "the sulphurous past," and again the name of Ibsen appeared, the only dramatist to be included among the novelists. Did not the Study, he asked, "preach Hardy and George Eliot and Jane Austen, Valdés, Galdós and Pardo-Bazán, Verga and Serao, Flaubert and the Goncourts and Zola, Björnson and Ibsen, Tourgénief and Dostoyevsky and Tolstoy, and Tolstoy, and even more Tolstoy, till its hearers slumbered in their pews?"

Though Howells commented on the plays of Shaw, Pinero, Wilde, and many more in "Life and Letters," which he wrote regularly for *Harper's Weekly* from 1895 to 1898, he observed in *My Literary Passions,* "I suppose I have not been a great reader of the drama." However, he tells us that by 1895 he had read all of Ibsen. Perhaps under the influence of the Norwegian, Howells wrote in *Harper's Weekly,* February 29, 1896, a plea for a national theater and argued that drama is "one of the most potent influences for good or evil in our lives . . . only less so than the novel itself . . . which is only a kind of portable theater." Ibsen, then, became for Howells a "canonized realist" who took his place among the Continental novelists in the Study, where Howells insistently thundered at the gates of "Fiction in Error."

The publication in 1889 in English of three of Ibsen's plays, *Ghosts, The Pillars of Society*, and *The Enemy of the People*, brought from the Study the first peal of thunder from Howells in defense of Ibsen. Before Howells' American readers had had an opportunity to see these plays presented on the stage, he seized upon them to prove once more the importance of the realistic movement sweeping across Europe. In the Study of May, 1889, he declared that the effect of Ibsen's plays is "not much less than tremendous," especially the play called *Ghosts*, "where the sins of the fathers are visibly visited upon the son." This play and others by Ibsen are "bitter with the most caustic irony, which is all the more mordant because it is so just." Howells quite clearly recognized that "there is often more of type than of character in his personages," that "the reality of the action is sometimes strained to an allegorical thinness," that the tone of the writing is frequently tame and flat; the plays, however, rise above their faults because of their truth to human experience. These dramas, banned in England, were being played in Europe, Howells assured his readers. We can only imagine, he said, the effect of Ibsen on the "fat optimism" of those who attend our theaters of New York only to be amused. "What our average audience would have to say of them we will not fancy."

The popularity in 1895 of a translation of Max Nordau's *Degeneration*, which "so many people are reading or making believe to read," again caused Howells to rise to the defense of one of Nordau's chief examples of "degeneracy"—Ibsen. In *Harper's Weekly*, April 13, Howells wrote a blistering attack on "the amusing madman," Dr. Max Nordau, "who fancies himself the only sane person in a world of lunatics." By chance Beerbohm Tree's presentation of *The Enemy of the People* was also under discussion in the spring of 1895, and the performance of the play added fuel to the fire already lit by Nordau's violent and ruthless attack on modern thought in general, especially as expressed by Ibsen, Tolstoy, and Zola. Two weeks after the review of Nordau's *Degeneration* Howells came to the defense of Ibsen in commenting on Beerbohm Tree's dramatic presentation. He found "a vast hope, a deep consolation" in the fact that Ibsen had at last been presented on the New York stage, "that haunt of the decrepitudes and imbecilities of the past." The performance gave Howells an experience in "absolute drama," because both actor and dramatist expressed "a most important conviction in ethics and in aesthetics." Just as Tolstoy reached his greatest effectiveness at the moment when ethics and aesthetics—truth and beauty—were perfectly balanced, so also did Ibsen. His drama became for Howells a "great theatrical event, the very greatest I have ever known," because it presented a social problem in terms of objective art. However, said Howells, the New York audience goes to the theater to be amused; there is "no love interest in the play" by Ibsen, no "action." Therefore, he concluded, "I am not thinking of any great acceptance for Ibsen himself on our stage, but for Ibsenism there is already great acceptance." Ibsen is "the master who has more to say to our generation in the theater than any other."

That the message of Ibsen proved too much for the New York audience of the 1890's, is indicated by the second selection printed below, a review of a performance of *Ghosts* in 1899. Remembering the impact of this drama on the New York audience of the 1890's, Howells wrote in the *North American Review*, July, 1906, after the death of Ibsen: "The great and dreadful delight of Ibsen is from his power of dispersing the conventional acceptations by which men live on easy terms with themselves, and obliging them to examine the grounds of their social and moral opinions."

A QUESTION OF PROPRIETY*

The latest performance of Ibsen's "Ghosts" in New York has been followed by quite as loud and long an outburst of wounded delicacy in public and private criticism as the earliest provoked. Now, as then, the play has been found immoral, pathological, and revolting; and if nothing else in the case is plain, it is plain that we are not yet used to the sort of extremes which it goes to.

We are used to almost every other imaginable sort of ex-

* *Literature*, July 7, 1899.

tremes in the theatre. There is hardly anything improper or repulsive which the stage has not shown, except the repulsive impropriety of "Ghosts," and the range outside of that play is so great that it is a little odd the author could not have been content with it. He might have deployed troops of women in lascivious dances with nothing between the audience and their nakedness except a thickness or a thinness of silken gauze; he might have left the scene strewn with shapes of mimic murder; he might have had false wives fooling jealous husbands, and coming back for a maudlin forgiveness; he might have had seducers spreading their lures for victims; he might have had repentant prostitutes dying in the last excesses of virtue and bringing reform to their lovers and remorse to their lovers' families; he might have had heroic thieves and highwaymen doing deeds of dazzling self-sacrifice; he might have had a noble and truthful gentleman wearing a mask of crime through four acts, and tearing it off in the fifth, barely in time to baffle villainy and rescue helpless innocence; he might have had a sister devoting herself to infamy, and taking the shame, in order to save a guilty sister's good name, or her husband's honor, or her children's feelings; he might have had a saintly suicide murdering himself, that his rival may marry the girl he loves; he might have had a girl contriving by every manner of lies the union of another with the man who adores her; he might have any or all of these abominable things, and offended no one. People are used to such things, and to any number of things like them, in the theatre, and if they are not disappointed when they do not get them, they certainly expect them.

But if all these traditions or none of them would have sufficed, there is the whole printed drama, from which the author might have chosen horrors freely, and without the least offence. There is no form of lust, adultery, incest, homicide, cruelty, deceit, which was not open to his choice in the Greek, Spanish, English, and French drama. One Elizabethan play, the "Hamlet" of William Shakespeare, is so infinitely rich in all these motives that Ibsen could have drawn upon it alone and had every revolting and depraving circumstance which he could reasonably desire, without the least offence. That is a play which we not only see without disgust, but with the highest intellectual pleasure, and, as we believe, with spiritual edification. It is never denounced by criticism for its loathsome fable, for its bloodshed, for the atrocity with which its hero breaks the heart of a gentle girl, or for the pathological spectacle of her madness and his own. Strangest of all, it is not condemned for leaving the witness in the same sort of uncertainty as to the specific lesson that he finds himself in at the end of "Ghosts."

The present high disdain for "Ghosts," then, must come simply from our unfamiliarity with the sort of means employed in it to strike terror. The means are novel, that is all; when they become stale and hackneyed; when we have them in the form of hash, as we are sure, finally, to have them, no one will object, and we shall be morally nourished by them, just as we are now morally nourished by those of "Hamlet." Then we may think no worse of the problem which a ghost leaves Mrs. Alving with regard to her son than of the problem which a ghost leaves Hamlet with regard to his mother. Possibly we may even come to think Mrs. Alving's problem is more important, as it is certainly more complex and profound. Compared with the question how she shall suffer to the end with the miserable boy whom his father's pleasant vices have doomed to idiocy, it is an easy matter for Hamlet to decide when and how to kill his uncle.

The psychological difference between the two tragedies is the measure of the vast space between the nerves of the seventeenth and the nineteenth centuries. In the nerves of the later time is the agonising consciousness of things unknown to the nerves of the earlier age; and it may be this tacit consciousness which recoils from the anguish of the touch laying it bare. It is not unimaginable that in some century yet to come, say the twenty-first or twenty-second, a like consciousness will recoil from a yet subtler analysis, and cry out for the good old, decent, wholesome, sanative, dramatic means employed in Ibsen's "Ghosts," as our consciousness now prefers to these the adulterous and vindictive motives of Shakespeare's "Hamlet." I can fancy an indignant and public-spirited criticism demanding the "scientific" methods of our then out-dated day as against those of some yet truer dramatist which shall hold the mirror still more unshrinkingly up to nature. That dramatist

will, of course, have his party, very much outnumbered and
ashamed, as Ibsen has his party in New York today; and I
wonder in what form of revolt against the prevailing criticism
this devoted little band will wreak its sense of injustice. Now,
one can say that compared to the spare, severe sufficiency of
"Ghosts," the romantic surplusage of "Hamlet" is as a Wagner
opera to a Greek tragedy; but what will the audacious partisan
of the future dramatist say in contrasting his work with that of
a then out-Ibsened Ibsen?

IBSENISM*

[Howells first comments on "four or five of the most characteristic of Ibsen's plays" presented in New York during the
previous five years and continues]:
    I am not thinking . . . of any great acceptance for Ibsen
himself on our stage, but for 'Ibsenism' there is already great
acceptance, and there will be greater and greater, for he is the
master who has more to say to our generation in the theatre
than any other, and all must learn his language who would be
understood hereafter. The chief trait of his speech, as I have
intimated, is its simplicity, and this has impressed itself upon
the diction of the new playwrights very noticeably already. Of
course, that sort of simplicity is a common tendency of our
time, but it is Ibsen who has felt it more than any other, and
who has, I think, imparted it in some measure to all who have
studied him. Both the theatre and the drama have studied Ibsen, and are studying him more and more: dramatic criticism
itself is deigning to look at him a little; but not nearly so much
as the drama and the theatre, perhaps because it need not;
like "genius" it knows without learning. The drama and the
theatre feel his simplicity in every way—his simplicity of
thought and sense, as well as his simplicity of speech. So far as
I have spoken with actors who have played Ibsen, I find that
without exception, almost, they like to play him, because he
gives them real emotions, real characters to express, and they

* *Harper's Weekly*, April 27, 1895.

feel in him the support of strong intentions. They have to forget a good deal that they have learned in the school of other dramatists. They have to go back, and become men and women again before Ibsen can do anything with them, or they with him; but when they have once done this, their advance toward a truer art than they have ever known is rapid and unerring. It is very interesting to hear a stage-manager, who has helped them remand themselves to this natural condition, talk of their difficulties in reaching it, when they are most willing and anxious to reach it. They have really to put away from them all that they have learned of artificial and conventional for the stage; everything but their technical skill is a loss, but this is an immense advantage, for Ibsen understands the stage, as perhaps no other dramatist has understood it; and in his knowledge and sympathy with the stage the actor feels a support which he can fully trust. He can implicitly believe that whatever he finds in the dialogue or the direction is fully and positively meant, and that he cannot go wrong if he is true to them. It is not possible to play Ibsen so badly as to spoil him if the actor obeys him; if he obeys him intelligently and skilfully the highest effect is unfailing; but if he merely obeys him blindly and ignorantly, a measure of success is sure to follow. For this reason I have never seen a play of Ibsen's which I felt to be a failure; the Réjane performance of the Doll's House was nearer a failure than any other, because the French stage seemed unwilling to obey Ibsen at all.

The influence of Ibsen on the theatre is very interesting, but it is not so important as his influence on the drama. I think the reader of Ibsen will be able to trace his influence in the work of any of the modern English playwrights, or at least I do not think I have deceived myself in imagining that I trace it in the plays of Mr. Pinero, or Mr. Shaw, or Mr. Jones. I do not mean that they have imitated him, or have slavishly followed him, but that they have learned from him a certain way of dealing with material; and I do not mean that they deal with life altogether as he does, or even largely, but only that each one does so in some degree. I could wish that they dealt with it altogether as he does in their choice of the problems they treat, or that they would treat such problems as concern conduct rather than such as concern action. The problem which a play of Ibsen hinges upon is as wide as the whole of life, and it seeks a solution in the conscience of the spectator for the future rather than the present; it is not an isolated case; it does not demand what he would do, or would have done, in a given event; and this is what makes the difference between him and the modern English playwrights. In morals, a puritanic narrowness cramps all our race, which will not suffer us to get beyond the question of personality; but Ibsen always transcends this, and makes you feel the import of what has happened civically, socially, humanly, universally. In *Ghosts*, for instance; who is to blame? You feel that nothing but the reconstitution of society will avail with the wrong and the evil involved.

But the new dramatists have learned from Ibsen to deal with questions of vital interest, and to deal with them naturally, and, on the whole, pretty honestly. For the rest, I should say that it would not be safe or just (what is unjust is never quite safe, I suppose) to say at which point you felt his influence. So much in the tendency of any time is a common effect from common causes, that it is not well to attribute this or that thing to this or that man. All the Elizabethan dramatists wrote somewhat like Shakespeare, and Shakespeare is the greatest of them all; and yet it would not be easy to prove that he was otherwise their master. I should not undertake to prove that the modern English drama was of the school of Ibsen, except as Ibsen is the greatest of the moderns. But I find much in the new plays that makes me think of him: situations, questions, treatment, motive, character, diction. They lack his poetry, but they have much of the same art, and it appears that we can get on without poetry in plays, but not without art. But whether they have their common traits in common with him because of their contemporaneity, and are like him because they are of the same century and the same modern circumstance, I am not ready to say; and so if I were really driven to the wall, and had to point out absolute instances of his influence in them or die, I should perhaps withdraw the word influence; and then go away thinking my own thoughts. He is above all a moralist, and they are all, more or less effectually, moralists both in the larger and the lesser sense.

Thomas Hardy (1840—1928)

Howells says in *My Literary Passions:* "I came rather late, but I came with all the ardor of what seems my perennial literary youth, to the love of Thomas Hardy, whom I first knew in his story, *A Pair of Blue Eyes.*" Since this novel appeared in 1873 and was not read by Howells until 1885 or 1886, we can only conclude that Howells had little hope for any fiction coming from England and therefore that he did not keep up with the current British books.

While Howells was still editor of the *Atlantic Monthly,* he missed the opportunity to include Hardy's name among his contributors. On September 6, 1879, Hardy wrote to James R. Osgood, owner of the magazine, suggesting that he write a serial for the *Atlantic.* Osgood showed the letter to Howells, but the editor—totally ignorant of Hardy's writing—made no proposal. Since *Far from the Madding Crowd* had already appeared in *Every Saturday,* edited by Howells' friend T. B. Aldrich, it is difficult to understand Howells' lapse, unless one remembers that he then considered Cambridge, Massachusetts, "the Elysian Fields," beyond which "there was very little good writing being done" in the English language.

Fortunately for Howells' own literary growth, he left the *Atlantic* in 1881 and journeyed to England, where he met Hardy through Edmund Gosse. It was after this visit of 1882-1883 and the return to Boston, "when I undertook a critical department in one of the magazines," that Howells read *A Pair of Blue Eyes.*

A letter "To Millicent from America" in *The Critic,* July 3, 1886, by an English traveler, Frederick Wedmore, shows that Howells continued to read and appreciate Hardy as one of the important writers of the day. Wedmore had luncheon with Howells and described him in the interview as

> a genial, downright, matter of fact, and withal satirical person—just now in the very fullest possession of his means, writing and talking with the utmost neatness, and without

the slightest effort. He talked much of books. . . . He agreed
with me very much when I praised Thomas Hardy. We
spoke particularly of "Under the Greenwood Tree" and "A
Pair of Blue Eyes." Still I can never forgive him for under-
rating Dickens.

Howells' attack on Dickens, one of the "passions" of his
childhood, was in fact an attack on romanticism in fiction
writing. In an interview reported in the *Critic* the following
year, Howells observed that Balzac, Gogol, and Dickens
"marked the inauguration of the realistic era by taking realities and placing them in romantic relations," but that all three
were essentially romantic. England, said Howells, stands "at
the very bottom of the list among the nations that have produced great modern novelists"—though, he added, "Hardy is a
great, I may say, a very great novelist. His pictures of life are
life itself."

The attitude that Howells had toward Hardy was well
known before the storm broke in this country in 1894 at the
appearance of *Jude the Obscure* as a serial in *Harper's*. The
excitement caused by *Jude* was described by J. Henry Harper
forty years later in *I Remember* (1934). Harper made a special trip to London to persuade Hardy to alter his story when,
to his editorial eyes, after the first few installments had appeared, "it looked a little squally." Hardy did, in fact, tone
down the objectionable sections for *Harper's*. The book, however, appeared in its entirety in November, 1895. Printed
below is Howells' enthusiastic review of *Jude the Obscure,*
which came out the following month in *Harper's Weekly,* one
day before Jeanette L. Gilder's review in the *New York
World* of December 8, in which she declared, "Thomas Hardy has scandalized the critics and shocked his friends."

Howells' support of Hardy never flagged. He reviewed the
stage version of *Tess of the D'Urbervilles* for *Harper's Weekly* in 1897, sent messages to Hardy by Hamlin Garland in
1899, included two essays on Hardy's women in *Heroines of
Fiction* (1901), and contributed several studies of Hardy's
poetry to the *North American Review.* Howells called on
Hardy when he visited England in 1910 and received a letter
of congratulation from the British novelist on the occasion of

his seventy-fifth birthday dinner. The personal relations of these two men remained unblemished for over twenty-five years. "I liked him," Hardy remarked of Howells to their common friend Hamlin Garland, "he was a good fellow."

Though Hardy was laconic on the subject of Howells, Howells has told us in *Heroines of Fiction* exactly what he thought of Hardy, whose very "faults" he grew to love. Hardy, like Björnson and Turgenev, Howells considered "a great poet as well as a great artist"; his plots are often artificial, even fantastic; his characters, especially his women, "wholly pagan," for "his people live very close to the heart of nature." But Hardy's "vision of humanity" was anything but romantic, and it was this that moved Howells to say of *Jude the Obscure,* "No greater or truer book has been written in our time or any."

PLEASURE FROM TRAGEDY*

It has never been quite decided yet, I believe, just what is the kind and what is the quality of pleasure we get from tragedy. A great many people have said what it is, but they seem not to have said this even to their own satisfaction. It is certain that we do get pleasure from tragedy, and it is commonly allowed that the pleasure we get from tragedy is nobler than the pleasure we get from comedy. An alloy of any such pleasure as we get from comedy is held to debase this finer emotion, but this seems true only as to the whole effect of tragedy. The Greek tragedy kept itself purely tragic; and English tragedy assimilated all elements of comedy and made them tragic; so that in the end Hamlet and Macbeth are as high sorrowful as Orestes and Oedipus.

I should be rather ashamed of lugging the classic and the romantic in here, if it were not for the sense I have of the return of an English writer to the Greek motive of tragedy in a book which seems to me one of the most tragical I have read.

* *Jude the Obscure,* by Thomas Hardy, 1895. Reviewed in *Harper's Weekly,* December 7, 1895.

I have always felt in Mr. Thomas Hardy a charm which I
have supposed to be that of the elder pagan world, but this I
have found in his lighter moods, for the most part, and
chiefly in his study of the eternal-womanly, surviving in certain unconscienced types and characters from a time before
Christianity was, and more distinctly before Puritanism was.
Now, however, in his latest work he has made me feel our
unity with that world in the very essence of his art. He has
given me the same pity and despair in view of the blind struggles of his modern English lower-middle-class people that I
experience from the destinies of the august figures of Greek
fable. I do not know how instinctively or how voluntarily he
has appealed to our inherent superstition of Fate, which used
to be a religion; but I am sure that in the world where his hap-
less people have their being, there is not only no Providence,
but there is Fate alone; and the environment is such that character itself cannot avail against it. We have back the old conception of an absolutely subject humanity, unguided and un-
friended. The gods, careless of mankind, are again over all;
only, now, they call themselves conditions.

The story is a tragedy, and tragedy almost unrelieved by
the humorous touch which the poet is master of. The grotesque is there abundantly, but not the comic; and at times
this ugliness heightens the pathos to almost intolerable effect.
But I must say that the figure of Jude himself is, in spite of all
his weakness and debasement, one of inviolable dignity. He is
the sport of fate, but he is never otherwise than sublime; he
suffers more for others than for himself. The wretched Sue
who spoils his life and her own, helplessly, inevitably, is the
kind of fool who finds the fool in the poet and prophet so often, and brings him to naught. She is not less a fool than Arabella herself; though of such exaltation in her folly that we
cannot refuse her a throe of compassion, even when she is
most perverse. All the characters, indeed, have the appealing
quality of human creatures really doing what they must while
seeming to do what they will. It is not a question of blaming
them or praising them; they are in the necessity of what they
do and what they suffer. One may indeed blame the author for
presenting such a conception of life; one may say that it is demoralizing if not immoral; but as to his dealing with his crea-

tions in the circumstance which he has imagined, one can only praise him for his truth.

The story has to do with some things not hitherto touched in fiction, or Anglo-Saxon fiction at least; and there cannot be any doubt of the duty of criticism to warn the reader that it is not for all readers. But not to affirm the entire purity of the book in these matters would be to fail of another duty of which there can be as little doubt. I do not believe any one can get the slightest harm from any passage of it; only one would rather that innocence were not acquainted with all that virtue may know. Vice can feel nothing but self-abhorrence in the presence of its facts.

The old conventional personifications seem drolly factitious in their reference to the vital reality of this strange book. I suppose it can be called morbid, and I do not deny that it is. But I have not been able to find it untrue, while I know that the world is full of truth that contradicts it. The common experience, or perhaps I had better say the common knowledge of life contradicts it. Commonly, the boy of Jude's strong aspiration and steadfast ambition succeeds and becomes in some measure the sort of man he dreamed of being. Commonly, a girl like Sue flutters through the anguish of her harassed and doubting youth and settles into acquiescence with the ordinary life of women, if not acceptance of it. Commonly, a boy like the son of Jude, oppressed from birth with the sense of being neither loved nor wanted, hardens himself against his misery, fights for the standing denied him, and achieves it. The average Arabella has no reversion to her first love when she has freed herself from it. The average Phillotson does not give up his wife to the man she says she loves, and he does not take her back knowing her loathing for himself. I grant all these things; and yet the author makes me believe that all he says to the contrary inevitably happened.

I allow that there are many displeasing things in the book, and few pleasing. Arabella's dimple-making, the pig-killing, the boy's suicide and homicide; Jude's drunken second marriage; Sue's wilful self-surrender to Phillotson: these and other incidents are revolting. They make us shiver with horror and grovel with shame, but we know that they are deeply founded in the condition, if not in the nature of humanity. There are besides these abhorrent facts certain accusations against some accepted formalities of civilization, which I suppose most readers will find hardly less shocking. But I think it is very well for us to ask from time to time the reasons of things, and to satisfy ourselves, if we can, what the reasons are. If the experience of Jude with Arabella seems to arraign marriage, and it is made to appear not only ridiculous but impious that two young, ignorant, impassioned creatures should promise lifelong fealty and constancy when they can have no real sense of what they are doing, and that then they should be held to their rash vow by all the forces of society, it is surely not the lesson of the story that any other relation than marriage is tolerable for the man and woman who live together. Rather it enforces the conviction that marriage is the sole solution of the question of sex, while it shows how atrocious and heinous marriage may sometimes be.

I find myself defending the book on the ethical side when I meant chiefly to praise it for what seems to me its artistic excellence. It has not only the solemn and lofty effect of a great tragedy; a work far faultier might impart this; but it has unity very uncommon in the novel, and especially the English novel. So far as I can recall its incidents there are none but such as seem necessary from the circumstances and the characters. Certain little tricks which the author sometimes uses to help himself out, and which give the sense of insincerity or debility, are absent here. He does not invoke the playful humor which he employs elsewhere. Such humor as there is tastes bitter, and is grim if not sardonic. This tragedy of fate suggests the classic singleness of means as well as the classic singleness of motive.

Emile Zola (1840—1902)

On March 18, 1882, Howells wrote to John Hay, "I am a great admirer of French workmanship, and I read everything of Zola's that I can lay hands on." When thirty years later Howells addressed the distinguished guests gathered to celebrate his seventy-fifth birthday, he said: "Some of you may not know this, but I know it, for I am of the generation that lived it and I would fain help to have it remembered that we studied from the French masters . . . to imitate nature, and gave American fiction the bent which it still keeps wherever it is vital."

Between these two dates, 1882 and 1912, Howells' admiration for Zola was frequently repeated in reviews, interviews, and letters. It is surprising, then, to note that though Howells had read *Page d'Amour* (1878) and *L'Assommoir* (1879) in French when they were first published, we find no reference in Howells' writing to Zola's *Roman experimental* (1880). It is difficult to believe that this important essay could have been overlooked by Howells, especially since it was discussed by Melchior de Vogüé, Valdés, Pardo-Bazán, Brander Matthews, and others in the decade before the appearance of *Criticism and Fiction*.

The next sentence in the letter to Hay—"But I have to hide the books from the children!"—suggests something of Howells' attitude toward Zola. It is well to remind ourselves that the critics mentioned above shuddered with Howells over Zola's naturalism, as did also Henry James, who visited Daudet, Goncourt, and Zola in Paris in 1884. "There is nothing more interesting to me now than the effort and experiment of this little group," James wrote to Howells in Boston, ". . . in spite of their ferocious pessimism and their handling of unclean things, they are at least serious and honest."

A similar hesitation on Howells' part about Zola is reflected in a letter "To Millicent from America," by Frederick Wedmore, who wrote that when he had luncheon with Howells in 1886,

We spoke of Zola, and when I extolled the "Page d'amour," he said it was certainly immense as a piece of pathos; though he sometimes doubted the motive a little—thought it a little forced—questioned whether the woman *would* have been quite so much in love with the doctor; whether the contest between her love for her child and the doctor would really have been quite so stubborn. "But in the matter of love, one can never say," and anyway it was immense as pathos.

Though Zola was under attack at this time both in Europe and America on moral grounds, Howells from the beginning recognized him as one of the great writers of the new school. Section XXIV of *Criticism and Fiction* indicates clearly the reservations Howells felt for "certain objectionable French novels." But from this censure Howells always made an exception of Zola, whom he placed by the side of Tolstoy and Ibsen. He perceived, however, that Zola was essentially a "romanticist," not a realist. Though Zola was distinctly not to be read by children, the real critical reservation to his naturalism was not moral but aesthetic—he was a romantic.

A year after the luncheon conversation with Wedmore, an enterprising young reporter from the *Tribune* followed Howells to his summer home in the Adirondacks and secured from him a long and interesting interview that appeared July 10, 1887. "Of course we all know the character of modern French writers," Howells said, but

Zola is a great writer. I may regret that he has concerned himself with the disagreeable and unhappy things of life, but I do not base my objection to him on that ground. Strange as it may seem, if I objected to him at all it would be that he was a romanticist. He is natural and true but he might better be more so. He has not quite escaped the influence of Balzac, who, with Dickens and Gogol, marked the inauguration of the realistic era by taking realities and placing them in romantic relations.

Later in the same interview Howells outlined what he called

"a true arrangement of literature, in which realism has obtained the supremacy over romance," and placed Russia first and "the French, by virtue of Zola's strength, second."

Early in the following year, in "The Editor's Study" of March, 1888, Howells addressed himself "to the reader of Zola's latest and perhaps awfulest book, *La Terre*," which had just appeared. Though Howells was disgusted by "the naked realities of lust and crime" that he found in the book, he insisted—in spite of the objections of the editor of *Harper's*—on printing the notice of *La Terre* that is reproduced below. Howells argued, at a time when French scholars such as Brunetière, Schérer, and Anatole France were attacking Zola, that *La Terre* should not be avoided by the student of civilization, but should instead be seriously considered, for "this tremendous charge against humanity," he said, must be faced.

Howells' insight into the essentially romantic character of the new naturalism tempered his appreciation of Zola's "epic greatness" in the single page he devoted to Zola in *My Literary Passions*. He had just read *L'Argent* (1891) with the same fascinated attention he had felt for *L'Assommoir* several years earlier and with the same abhorrence for the material of the novel. But "the critics know now," he wrote, "that Zola is not the realist he used to fancy himself, and he is full of the best qualities of the romanticism he has hated so much; but for what he is, there is but one novelist of our time, or of any, that outmasters him, and that is Tolstoy."

The names of Ibsen, Zola, and Tolstoy were linked in Howells' mind; though each of these literary figures was to him a unique genius, together they reflected the vigor of the century then drawing to a close.

Following Howells' review of *La Terre* is part of his review of Max Nordau's *Degeneration*. In these paragraphs Howells, with insight heightened by indignation, defines the individual gifts of Ibsen, Tolstoy, and Zola, and the importance to modern civilization of their united attack on the shams and evasions of the period.

A few weeks after the death of Zola in 1902, Howells' essay "Émile Zola," appeared in the *North American Review*. In it Howells observed that "a poet of such great epical imagination, such great ethical force, as Émile Zola may be seen

as clearly and judged as fairly immediately after his death as
he will be by posterity." Having passed beyond the sound of
the furor over realism in the 1890's, he reiterated the critical creed achieved in his years in the Study and concluded
that Zola "conceived of reality poetically" (that is to say, ro-
mantically); that he was "an artist, and one of the greatest,
but even before and beyond that he was intensely a moralist."
"The ethics of his work, like that of Tolstoy's, were always
carrying over into his life," and when "an act of public and
official atrocity," such as the Dreyfus case, "disturbed the
working of his mind and revolted his nature, he could not
rest again till he had done his best to right it." Though Zola's
literary success "has its imperfections," inasmuch as he was
bred and nourished a romanticist, "his success as a humanist
is without flaw."

ZOLA'S NATURALISM*

There is in the course of history something more than the suggestion that evil dies of the mortal sting which it inflicts, and
that it defeats those who employ it, in accomplishing itself. . . .

In the mean time some of the questions involved will present themselves to the reader of Zola's latest and perhaps awfulest book, *La Terre*. Filthy and repulsive as it is in its facts,
it is a book not to be avoided by the student of civilization,
but rather to be sought and seriously considered. It is certainly not a book for young people, and it is not a book for any
one who cares merely for a story, or who finds himself by experience the worse for witnessing in literature the naked realities of lust and crime. This said, it is but fair to add that it
legitimately addresses itself to scientific curiosity and humane
interest. The scene passes in that France where the first stirring of a personal conscience once promised a brilliant race
the spiritual good which triumphant persecution finally de-

* *La Terre*, by Emile Zola, 1888. Reviewed in *Harper's Monthly*,
March, 1888.

nied it; and it is not wholly gratuitous to suppose that we see
in the peasants of *La Terre* effects of the old repressions
which stifled religious thought among them, and bound all
their hopes, desires, and ambitions to the fields they tilled.
When the Revolution came, it came too late to undo the evil
accomplished, and the immediate good that it did included
another evil. It justly gave to the peasant the ownership of the
land, but it implanted in him the most insatiable earth-hunger
ever known in the world. This creature, this earth-fiend whom
Zola paints, is superstitious, but cynically indifferent to religion, and apparently altogether unmoral; lustful and un-
chaste, but mostly saved from the prodigal vices by avarice
that spares nothing, relents to no appeal, stops at no wrong,
and aspires only to the possession of land, and more land, and
ever more land. This is the prevailing type, varied and relieved by phases of simple, natural good in a few of the characters; and the Church, so potent against the ancestral heresy,
struggles in vain against the modern obduracy, in the character of the excellent priest, who is the only virtuous person in
the book. The story is a long riot of satyr-lewdness and satyr-
violence, of infernal greed that ends in murder, of sordid
jealousies and cruel hates; and since with all its literary power, its wonderful force of realization, it cannot remain valuable as literature, but must have other interest as a scientific
study of a phase of French life under the Second Empire, it
seems a great pity it should not have been fully documented.
What are the sources, the proofs, of this tremendous charge
against humanity, in those simple conditions, long fabled the
most friendly to the simple virtues? This is the question
which the reader, impatient if not incredulous of all this horror, asks himself when he has passed through it.

He must ask it also at the end of that curious narrative
drama of Tolstoi's known to us as yet only in the French version of *La Puissance des Ténèbres*. This too deals with peasant life, and with much the same hideous shames and crimes
as *La Terre*. The main difference—but it is a very great one—
is that the Russian peasant, wicked as he is, is not so depraved
as the French peasant; he has a conscience; he is capable of
remorse, of repentance, of expiation. . . . We should again,

however, like to have the documentary proofs in the case, and should feel more hopeful of the good to be done among the muzhiks by the play if we felt sure that they would recognize it as a true picture. In the mean time they are not likely to know much about it; the censorship has forbidden its representation in Russia, and it remains for the consideration of such people of other countries as know how to read.

Whether much is done to help those whose life is depicted in fiction is a question which no one is yet qualified to answer, fiction has only so very recently assumed to paint life faithfully, and most critics claim that it is best for it not to do so.

DEGENERATION*

[In the first two sections of Howells' review of *Degeneration*, by Max Nordau, he points out that the author is neither profound nor original. Howells denies that the civilization of the West is, at the end of the century, declining. Sections III, IV, and V follow.]

The world, in its thinking and feeling, was never so sound and sane before. There is a great deal of fevered and foolish thinking and feeling about thinking and feeling, as there always has been and will be, but there is no more of it than ever. It is no part of my business to defend the nineteenth century, and if I thought the noble mood of its last years merely a death-bed repentance, and not an effect of all the former events of the ages, I should not rejoice in it. Dr. Nordau himself is able to see that there really is no such thing as a *fin de siècle* spirit; but the race is in a certain mood, and the century is near its end, and so the phrase serves as well as another. The only question is whether the mood is a good one, and I have already expressed my sense of it.

I believe it is extremely well to have the underpinning of sentiment and opinion examined, from time to time, and this is what our age above all others has done. It is not a con-

---

* *Degeneration,* by Max Nordau, translated, 1895. Reviewed in *Harper's Weekly,* April 13, 1895.

structive or a reconstructive age, as compared with some other epochs, but it is eminently critical, and whatever is creative in it, is critically creative. It is very conscious, it not only knows, but it keenly feels, what it is about. It is not for nothing, it is not blindly or helplessly that it has tried this or that, that it has gone forward to new things or reverted to old things. It experiments perpetually, but not empirically; knowledge and greater knowledge are the cause and the effect of all that it has done in the arts as well as in the sciences.

If we stand at the end of things, we also stand at the beginning; we are the new era as well as the old. It is not at all important that certain things have fulfilled themselves and passed away; but it is very important that certain others have just begun their fulfillment, and it is these that we are to judge our time by. Our condition is that of a youth and health unknown to human thought before, and it is an excellent thing that with these we have so much courage; if it were only the courage of youth and health it would be well; but it is in fact the courage of a soul that is as old as the world.

A great many good, elderly minded people think it dreadful Ibsen should show us that the house we have lived in so long is full of vermin, that its drainage is bad, that the roof leaks and the chimney smokes abominably; but if it is true, is it not well for us to know it? It is dreadful because it is so, not because he shows it so; and the house is no better because our fathers got on in it as it is. He has not done his work without showing his weakness as well as his strength, and as I do not believe in genius in the miraculous sense, I am not at all troubled by his occasional weakness. It is really no concern of mine whether he solves his problems or not; generally, I see that he does not solve them, and I see that life does not; the longer I live the more I am persuaded that the problems of this life are to be solved elsewhere, or never. It is not by the solution of problems that the moralist teaches, but by the question that his handling of them suggests to us respecting ourselves. Artistically he is bound, Ibsen as a dramatist is bound, to give an aesthetic completeness to his works, and I do not find that he ever fails to do this; to my thinking they have a high beauty and propriety; but ethically he is bound not to be final; for if he forces himself to be final in things

that do not and cannot end here, he becomes dishonest, he
becomes a Nordau. What he can and must do ethically, is to
make us take thought of ourselves, and look to it whether we
have in us the making of this or that wrong, whether we are
hypocrites, tyrants, pretenders, shams conscious or unconscious; whether our most unselfish motives are not really secret shapes of egotism; whether our convictions are not mere
brute acceptations; whether we believe what we profess;
whether when we force good to a logical end we are not doing evil. This is what Ibsen does; he gives us pause; and in
that bitter muse he leaves us thinking not of his plays, but of
our own lives; not of his fictitious people, but of ourselves. If
we find ourselves all right we can go ahead with a good conscience, but never quite so cocksure afterwards.

He does in the region of motive pretty much the same work
that Tolstoi does in the region of conduct. If he makes you
question yourself before God, Tolstoi makes you question
yourself before man. With the one you ask yourself, Am I
true? With the other you ask yourself, Am I just? You cannot
release yourself from them on any other terms. They will
neither of them let you go away, feeling smoothly self-satis-
fied, patronizingly grateful, smugly delighted, quite charmed.
If you want that feeling, you must go to some other shop
for it, and there are shops a plenty where you can get it. Both
of these great writers now and then overrun each other's province, for their provinces are not very separable, except by a
feat of the fancy, though if the reader wishes a distinction between them, I have offered one. I should say, however, that
Ibsen dealt with conduct in the ideal, and Tolstoi in the real.
How shall I behave with regard to myself? How shall I behave with regard to my neighbor? I imagine that in either
case the answer would be the same. It is only the point of
view that is different.

As far as any finality is concerned, Tolstoi is no more satis-
factory than Ibsen; that is to say, he is quite as honest. He
does not attempt to go beyond Christ, who bade us love the
neighbor, and cease to do evil; but I suppose this is what
Dr. Nordau means by his mysticism, his sentimentality. In
fact, Tolstoi has done nothing more than bring us back to the
gospels as the fountain of righteousness. Those who denounce

him cannot or will not see this, but that does not affect the fact. He asks us to be as the first Christians were, but this is difficult, and it has been so difficult ever since the times of the first Christians, that very few of the later Christians have been at all like them. Even in his most recent crusade, his crusade against the chauvinism which we miscall patriotism, he only continues that warfare against the spirit of provinciality which Christianity began. He preaches no new doctrine, he practices no new life. It is all as old as Calvary; it is the law and life of self-sacrifice. This was and always will be to the Jews a stumbling-block, and to the Greeks foolishness; but it is nothing mystical. There is nothing mystical in Tolstoï's books; as far as they are fictions they are the closest and clearest transcripts of the outer and inner life of man; as far as they are lessons in the form of allegory or essay, they are of the simplest and plainest meaning. His office in the world has been like Ibsen's, to make us look where we are standing, and see whether our feet are solidly planted or not. What is our religion, what is our society, what is our country, what is our civilization? You cannot read him without asking yourself these questions, and the result is left with you. Tolstoï's solution of the problem in his own life is not the final answer, and as things stand it is not the possible answer. We cannot all go dig in the fields, we cannot all cobble peasants' shoes. But we can all do something to lift diggers and cobblers to the same level with ourselves, to see that their work is equally rewarded, and that they share fully with the wisest and the strongest in the good of life. We can get off their backs, or try to get off, and this, after all, is what Tolstoï means us to do.

There is the same mixture of weakness in his power that qualifies the power of Ibsen, and makes his power the more admirable. There are flaws enough in his reasoning; he is not himself the best exponent of his own belief; there is no finality in his precept or his practice. On the other hand, his work has the same aesthetic perfection as Ibsen's, and as an intellect dealing imaginatively with life, he is without a rival. There is the like measure of weakness in Zola, whom Dr. Nordau chooses as the type of realist, with much the same blundering wilfulness that he chooses Ibsen as the type of egomaniac, and Tolstoi as the type of mystic. Zola never was a realist in the right sense, and no one has known this better, or has said it more frankly than Zola himself. He is always showing, as he has often owned that he came too early to be a realist; but it was he who imagined realism, in all its sublime, its impossible beauty, as Ibsen imagined truth, as Tolstoi imagined justice. One has to deal with words that hint rather than say what one means, but the meaning will be clear enough to any one capable of giving the matter thought. What Zola has done has been to set before us an ideal of realism, to recall the wandering mind of the world to that ideal, which was always in the world, and to make the reader feel it by what he has tried to do, rather than by what he has done. He has said, in effect, You must not aim in art to be less than perfectly faithful; and you must not lie about the fact any more than you can help. Go to life; see what it is like, and then tell it as honestly as possible. Above all he has shown us what rotten foundations the most of fiction rested on, and how full of malaria the whole region was. He did not escape the infection himself; he was born in that region; the fever of romanticism was in his blood; the taint is in his work. But he has written great epics, and the time will come when it will be seen that he was the greatest poet of his day, and perhaps the greatest poet that France has produced.

Leo Tolstoy (1828—1910)

Since Tolstoy remained to Howells the master among all his European masters, the selections for Part I will conclude with Howells' matured judgment of Tolstoy rather than with his early reviews. The essay chosen was written in 1897 for *A Library of the World's Best Literature,* under the editorship of Howells' friend, Charles Dudley Warner. Howells' early enthusiasm for the Russian novelist, whom he read for the first time in 1885, began more than a decade before the writing of the essay. "As much as one merely human being can help another I believe that he has helped me," is Howells' simple statement in *My Literary Passions* of the effect on him of Tolstoy's writings. He then adds the significant comment, "He has not influenced me in esthetics only, but in ethics, too, so that I can never again see life in the way I saw it before I knew him." It is for the reader to determine, if he can, the part played by Tolstoy in the formulation of Howells' literary criticism after 1885, when the tone of his reviews was deepened by ethical and social considerations.

In an essay on Tolstoy in the *North American Review* (December, 1908), Howells tells that he first saw *My Religion* and *War and Peace* in a French translation when visiting "two valued friends" in Cambridge. "Seven or eight years" later Howells, at the age of fifty, began the reading of *The Cossacks,* which had been in his possession, though unread, for "four or five years." To T. S. Perry, on October 30, 1885, Howells wrote, *"Anna Karénine* is a wonderful book." Though English translations of Tolstoy began to appear in this country between 1885 and 1887, Howells read *Anna Karenine* in French, and he reviewed the novel, together with *My Religion* and *Scenes of the Siege of Sebastopol,* in "The Editor's Study" of April, 1886. The following February he reviewed in the same magazine the French translations of Tolstoy's *Deux Générations* and *La Mort d'Ivan Illitch,* the effects of which, he told his readers, are "as deep and broad, as far-reaching as in a tragedy of Shakespeare."

Two books from which Howells derived much of his knowledge of Tolstoy, concerning whom he wrote an essay for *Harper's Weekly*, April 23, 1887, are *Les Grandes Maîtres de la Littérature Russe*, by Ernest Dupuy, and *La Roman Russe*, by Eugène-Melchior de Vogüé (see "Editor's Study," November, 1886). Both books had appeared in France several years earlier and had played an important part in the "Russomania" of that country. M. Dupuy's study contains long biographical essays on Gogol, Turgenev, and Tolstoy; M. de Vogüé's more brilliant essays, which had previously appeared between 1883 and 1886 in the *Revue des Deux Mondes*, added Dostoevski to the list and also included a comparison of Russian realism and French naturalism. Through his review of these two books Howells made his espousal of Tolstoy part of the larger critical argument of the decade. As he was urging a redefinition of realism against the defenders of the falsely romantic in this country, so the French critics presented the Russian novelist to their readers in opposition to exaggerated naturalism as defined by Zola's *Roman experimental* (1880), which seemed to them coarse and materialistic.

By April, 1887, when Howells wrote for *Harper's Weekly* the essay on Tolstoy, he had become an avowed Tolstoyan. The Russian was to Howells at that time "precisely the human being" with whom he found himself "in greatest intimacy," not, he added, through personal contact, but because he knew himself through Tolstoy. Howells freely acknowledged the influence on him at this time of *The Cooperative Commonwealth*, by Laurence Gronlund; of the *Fabian Essays;* of William Morris' tracts; of Bellamy's *Looking Backward;* but, he concluded, "the greatest influence . . . came to me through reading Tolstoy." This influence was deepened by Howells' contact with the Christian Socialists of Boston, who were also followers of the Russian novelist.

Howells' many comments, reviews, and essays on Tolstoy that appeared in magazines and newspapers during the last decades of the nineteenth century and the first of the twentieth show that his devotion to this "master" never wavered. In 1890 John Wanamaker, the Postmaster General, prohibited the mailing of Tolstoy's *Kreutzer Sonata*. Replying to the discussion aroused by this action, Howells pointed out in "The Editor's Study," October, 1890, "the inexorable truth" of Tolstoy's story, given the character of the hero. He repudiated, however, Tolstoy's "Afterword," in which the author admitted that the hero's views were his own. The reading of Tolstoy remained to Howells a "religious experience," in spite of Tolstoy's views on marriage expressed in his "deplorable reply." In 1914, in a conversation with Joyce Kilmer, Howells remarked: "I never met Tolstoy. But I once sent him a message of appreciation after he had sent a message to me. Tolstoy's force is a moral force. His great art is as simple as nature."

The lesson Howells seems to have derived from Tolstoy, then, is that the moral force of such a writer is greater than any rules of art. It is for this reason that Howells placed Tolstoy above Turgenev, as he tells us in *My Literary Passions:* "I thought the last word in literary art had been said to me by the novels of Tourguenif, but it seemed like the first, merely, when I began to acquaint myself with the simpler method of Tolstoy." Turgenev taught Howells the art of novel writing; Tolstoy taught him to be impatient "even of the artifice that hides itself" and to seek only "the incomparable truth" beneath the tale.

Exactly what this Tolstoyan truth was to Howells he tells us, as nearly as he can, when he says that Tolstoy taught him to see life not as the pursuit of personal happiness but as "a field for endeavor toward the happiness of the whole human family." Through Tolstoy, and the Christian Socialists, Howells recognized the meaning of the life of Christ with "a rapture such as I have known in no other reading." How Howells equated the new realism with the truth of Christianity, on which he felt that democracy in the true sense was based, can be traced in his essay "Lyof Tolstoi." He wrote this essay at a time in his own development when his enthusiasm for Tolstoy had in no way abated, and the place Tolstoy was to occupy in his own hierarchy of values was most finely felt. Tolstoy for

Howells became the basis not only of the literary, but also of the social and religious, dreams for this country, which underlies the thought of *Criticism and Fiction*.

Both ethically and aesthetically, Howells tells us, Tolstoy showed him a greatness that the Russian could never teach his American admirer. Though Howells disclaimed any effect of "the giant strides" of Tolstoy in the "pace" of his own writing—"I think that I had determined what I had to do before I read any Russian novels"—one cannot fail to observe that his concept of "complicity," which he first expressed in *The Minister's Charge* (1887), then in *Annie Kilburn* (1889), and later in *A Hazard of New Fortunes* (1890), reflects his understanding of the interrelation of the "whole human family," upon which he was led to meditate more deeply by his reading of Tolstoy. These ideas Howells had discussed with a group of like-minded men and women during his two years in Boston, 1889-1891, and had expressed again in *A Traveler from Altruria* and *A World of Chance*. In the following essay Howells gives full expression to what at the turn of the century Tolstoy finally meant to him.

THE PHILOSOPHY OF TOLSTOY*

There is a certain unsatisfactory meagreness in the facts of Lyof Tolstoy's life, as they are given outside of his own works. In these he has imparted himself with a fullness which has an air almost of anxiety to leave nothing unsaid,—as if any reticence would rest like a sense of insincerity on his conscience. But such truth as relates to dates and places, and seems the basis of our knowledge concerning other men, is with him hardly at all structural: we do not try to build his moral or intellectual figure upon it or about it.

He is of an aristocratic lineage, which may be traced back to Count Piotr Tolstoy, a friend and comrade of Peter the Great; and he was born in 1828 at Yasnaya Polyana near

---

* From *The Library of the World's Best Literature*, ed. R. S. Peale and J. A. Hill, 1897.

Tula, where he still lives. His parents died during his childhood, and he was left with their other children to the care of one of his mother's relatives at Kazan, where he entered the university. He did not stay to take a degree, but returned to Yasnaya Polyana, where he lived in retirement till 1851; when he went into the army, and served in the Caucasus and the Crimea, seeing both the big wars and the little. He quitted the service with the rank of division commander, and gave himself up to literary work at St. Petersburg, where his success was in every sort most brilliant; but when the serfs were set free, he retired to his estates, and took his part in fitting them for freedom by teaching them, personally and through books which he wrote for them.

He learned from these poor people far more than he taught them; and his real life dates from his efforts to make it one with their lives. He had married the daughter of a German physician in Moscow,—the admirable woman who has remained constant to the idealist through all his changing ideals,—and a family of children was growing up about him; but neither the cares nor the joys of his home sufficed to keep him from the despair which all his military and literary and social success had deepened upon him, and which had begun to oppress him from the earliest moments of moral consciousness.

The wisdom that he learned from toil and poverty was, that life has no meaning and no happiness except as it is spent for others; and it did not matter that the toiling poor themselves illustrated the lesson unwittingly and unwillingly. Tolstoy perceived that they had the true way often in spite of themselves; but that their reluctance or their ignorance could not keep the blessing from them which had been withheld from him, and from all the men of his kind and quality. He found that they took sickness and misfortune simply and patiently, and that when their time came to die, they took death simply and patiently. To them life was not a problem or a puzzle; it was often heavy and hard, but it did not mock or deride them; it was not malign, it was not ironical. He believed that the happiness he saw in them came first of all from their labor.

So he began to work out his salvation with his own hands.

He put labor before everything else in his philosophy, and
through all his changes and his seeming changes he has kept
it there. There had been a time when he thought he must destroy himself, after glory in arms and in letters had failed to
suffice him, after the love of wife and children had failed to
console him, and nothing would ease the intolerable burden
of being. But labor gave him rest; and he tasted the happiness
of those whose existence is a continual sacrifice through service to others.

He must work hard every day, or else he must begin to die
at heart; and so he believes must every man. But then, for the
life which labor renders tolerable and significant, some sort
of formulated faith was essential; and Tolstoy began to search
the Scriptures.[4] He learned from the teachings of Jesus Christ
that he must not only not kill, but he must not hate or despise
other men; he must not only keep himself chaste, but he
must keep his thoughts from unchastity; he must not only
not forswear himself, but he must not swear at all; he must
not only not do evil, but he must not *resist* evil. If his own
practice had been the negation of these principles, he could
not therefore deny their righteousness; if all civilization, as
we see it now, was the negation of these principles, civilization—in so far as it was founded upon war, and pride, and
luxury, and oaths, and judgments, and punishments—was
wrong and false. The sciences, so far as they failed to better
the lot of common men, seemed to him futile; the fine arts, so
far as they appealed to the passions, seemed worse than futile;
the mechanic arts, with their manifold inventions, were senseless things in the sight of this seer, who sought the kingdom
of God. Titles, honors, riches; courts, judges, executioners;
nationalities, armies, battles; culture, pleasure, amusement,—
he counted these all evil or vain.

The philosophy of Tolstoy is neither more nor less than the
doctrine of the gospels, chiefly as he found it in the words of
Jesus. Some of us whose lives it accused, have accused him of
going beyond Christ in his practice of Christ's precepts. We
say that having himself led a worldly, sensual, and violent
life, he naturally wished to atone for it by making every one
also lead a poor, dull, and ugly life. It is no part of my busi-

ness to defend him, or to justify him; but as against this anger
against him, I cannot do less than remind the reader that
Tolstoy, in confessing himself so freely and fully to the world,
and preaching the truth as he feels it, claims nothing like in-
fallibility. He compels no man's conscience, he shapes no
man's conduct. If the truth which he has learned from the
teachings of Jesus, and those other saviors and sages whom he
follows less devotedly, compels the conscience and shapes the
conduct of the reader, that is because this reader's soul cannot
deny it. If the soul rejects it, that is no more than men have
been doing ever since saviors and sages came into the world;
and Tolstoy is neither to praise nor to blame.

No sincere person, I believe, will deny his sincerity, which
is his authority outside of the gospel's: if any man will speak
simply and truly to us, he masters us; and this and nothing
else is what makes us helpless before the spirit of such books
as "My Confession," "My Religion," "Life," "What to Do,"
and before the ethical quality of Tolstoy's fictions. We can remind ourselves that he is no more final than he pretends to
be; that on so vital a point as the question of a life hereafter,
he seems of late to incline to a belief in it, though at first he
held such a belief to be a barbarous superstition. We can justly say that he does not lead a life of true poverty if his wife
holds the means of keeping him from want, and from that
fear of want which is the sorest burden of poverty. We can
point out that his labor in making shoes is a worse than useless travesty, since it may deprive some wretched cobbler of
his chance to earn his living by making and selling the shoes
which Count Tolstoy makes and gives away. In these things
we should have a certain truth on our side; though we should
have to own that it was not his fault that he had not really
declassed himself, and was constrained to the economic safety
in which he dwells. We should have to confess that in this the
great matter is the will; and that if benevolence stopped to
take account of the harm it might work, there could be no
such thing as charity in the world. We should have to ask ourselves whether Tolstoy's conversion to a belief in immortality
is not an effect of his unselfish labor; whether his former doubt
of immortality was not a lingering effect of the ambition, van-

ity, and luxury he has renounced. It had not indeed remained for him to discover that whenever we love, the truth is added unto us; but possibly it had remained for him to live the fact, to realize that unselfish labor gives so much meaning to human life that its significance cannot be limited to mortality.

However this may be, Tolstoy's purpose is mainly to make others realize that religion, that Christ, is for this actual world here, and not for some potential world elsewhere. If this is what renders him so hateful to those who postpone the Divine justice to another state of being, they may console themselves with the reflection that his counsel to unselfish labor is almost universally despised. There is so small danger that the kingdom of heaven will come by virtue of his example, that none of all who pray for it need be the least afraid of its coming. In any event his endeavor for a right life cannot be forgotten. Even as a pose, if we are to think so meanly of it as that, it is by far the most impressive spectacle of the century. All that he has said has been the law of Christianity open to any who would read, from the beginning; and he has not differed from most other Christians except in the attempt literally to do the will of Christ. Yet even in this he is not the first. Others have lived the life of labor voluntarily, and have abhorred war, and have suffered evil. But no man so gloriously gifted and so splendidly placed has bowed his neck and taken the yoke upon it. We must recognize Tolstoy as one of the greatest men of all time, before we can measure the extent of his renunciation. He was gifted, noble, rich, famous, honored, courted; and he has done his utmost to become plebeian, poor, obscure, neglected. He has truly endeavored to cast his lot with the lowliest, and he has counted it all joy so far as he has succeeded. His scruple against constraining the will of others suffers their will to make his self-sacrifice finally histrionic; but this seems to me not the least part of his self-sacrifice, which it gives a supreme touch of pathos. It is something that in fiction he alone could have imagined, and is akin to the experience of his own Karénin, who in a crucial moment forgives when he perceives that he cannot forget without being ridiculous. Tolstoy, in allowing his family to keep his wealth, for fear of compelling them to the righteousness which they do not choose, becomes absurd in his inalienable safety and superiority; but we cannot say that he ought not to suffer this indignity. There is perhaps a lesson in his fate which we ought not to refuse, if we can learn from it that in our time men are bound together so indissolubly that every advance must include the whole of society, and that even self-renunciation must not accomplish itself at the cost of others' free choice.

It is usual to speak of the ethical and the aesthetical principles as if they were something separable; but they are hardly even divergent in any artist, and in Tolstoy they have converged from the first. He began to write at a time when realistic fiction was so thoroughly established in Russia that there was no question there of any other. Gogol had found the way out of the mists of romanticism into the open day, and Turguénief had so perfected the realistic methods that the subtlest analysis of character had become the essence of drama. Then Tolstoy arrived, and it was no longer a question of methods. In Turguénief, when the effect sought and produced is most ethical, the process is so splendidly aesthetical that the sense of its perfection is uppermost. In Tolstoy the meaning of the thing is so supreme that the delight imparted by the truth is qualified by no consciousness of the art. Up to his time fiction had been part of the pride of life, and had been governed by the criterions of the world which it amused. But he replaced the artistic conscience by the human conscience. Great as my wonder was at the truth in Tolstoy's work, my wonder at the love in it was greater yet. Here for the first time, I found the most faithful pictures of life set in the light of that human conscience which I had falsely taught myself was to be ignored in questions of art, as something inadequate and inappropriate. In the august presence of the masterpieces, I had been afraid and ashamed of the highest instincts of my nature as something philistine and provincial. But here I stood in the presence of a master, who told me not to be afraid or ashamed of them, but to judge his work by them, since he had himself wrought in honor of them. I found the tests of conduct which I had used in secret with myself, applied as the rules of universal justice, condemning and acquitting in motive and action, and admitting none of those lawyers' pleas which baffle our own consciousness of right and wrong. Often in Tolstoy's ethics I feel a hardness, almost an arrogance (the word says too much); but in his aesthetics I have never felt this. He has transmuted the atmosphere of a realm hitherto supposed unmoral into the very air of heaven. I found nowhere in his work those base and cruel lies which cheat us into the belief that wrong may sometimes be right through passion, or genius, or heroism. There was everywhere the grave noble face of the truth that had looked me in the eyes all my life, and that I knew I must confront when I came to die. But there was something more than this,—infinitely more. There was that love which is before even the truth, without which there is no truth, and which, if there is any last day, must appear the Divine justice.

It is Tolstoy's humanity which is the grace beyond the reach of art in his imaginative work. It does not reach merely the poor and the suffering: it extends to the prosperous and the proud, and does not deny itself to the guilty. There had been many stories of adultery before "Anna Karénina,"—nearly all the great novels outside of English are framed upon that argument,—but in "Anna Karénina" for the first time the whole truth was told about it. Tolstoy has said of the fiction of Maupassant that the truth can never be immoral; and in his own work I have felt that it could never be anything but moral. In the "Kreutzer Sonata,"[5] which gave a bad conscience to Christendom, there was not a moment of indecency or horror that was not purifying and wholesome. It was not the logic of that tremendous drama that marriage was wrong,—though Tolstoy himself pushed on to some such conclusion,—but only that lustful marriage, provoked through appetite and fostered in idleness and luxury, was wrong. We may not have had the last word from him concerning the matter: he may yet see marriage, as he has seen immortality, to be the inevitable deduction from the human postulate. But whatever his mind about it may finally be, his comment[6] on that novel seems to me his one great mistake, and a discord in the harmony of his philosophy.

It jars the more because what you feel most in Tolstoy is

this harmony,—this sense of unity. He cannot admit in his arraignment of civilization the plea of a divided responsibility: he will not suffer the prince, or the judge, or the soldier, personally to shirk the consequences of what he officially does; and he refuses to allow in himself the division of the artist from the man. As I have already more than once said, his ethics and aesthetics are inseparably at one; and this is what gives a vital warmth to all his art. It is never that heartless skill which exists for its own sake, and is content to dazzle with the brilliancy of its triumphs. It seeks always the truth in the love to which alone the truth unveils itself. If Tolstoy is the greatest imaginative writer who ever lived, it is because, beyond all others, he has written in the spirit of kindness, and not denied his own personal complicity with his art.

As for the scope of his work, it would not be easy to measure it; for it seems to include all motives and actions, in good and bad, in high and low, and not to leave life untouched at any point as it shows itself in his vast Russian world. Its chief themes are the old themes of art always,—they are love, passion, death; but they are treated with such a sincerity, such a simplicity, that they seem almost new to art, and as effectively his as if they had not been touched before.

Until we read "The Cossacks," and witness the impulses of kindness in Olenin, we do not realize how much love has been despised by fiction, and neglected for passion. It is with a sort of fear and trembling that we find ourselves in the presence of this wish to do good to others, as if it might be some sort of mawkish sentimentality. But it appears again and again in the cycle of Tolstoy's work: in the vague aspirations recorded in "Childhood, Boyhood, and Youth"; in the abnegation and shame of the husband in "Anna Karénina," when he wishes to forgive his wife's paramour; in the goodness of the *muzhik* to the loathsome sick man in "The Death of Ivan Ilyitch"; in the pitying patience of Prince Andreí Bolkonsky with Anatol Kuragin in "War and Peace," where amidst his own anguish he realizes that the man next him under the surgeon's knife is the wretch who robbed him of the innocent love of his betrothed; in the devotion of the master, even to the mergence of conscious identity, to the servant in "Master and Man";—

and at no time does it justify our first skeptical shrinking. It is as far as possible from the dramatic *tours de force* in Hugo-esque fiction; it is not a conclusion that is urged or an effect that is solicited: it is the motive to which all beauty of action refers itself; it is human nature,—and it is as frankly treated as if there could be no question of it.

This love—the wish to do good and to be good, which is at the bottom of all our hearts, however we try to exclude it or deny it—is always contrasting itself in Tolstoy's work with passion, and proving the latter mortal and temporal in itself, and enduring only in its union with love. In most other novelists, passion is treated as if it were something important in itself,—as if its intensity were a merit and its abandon were a virtue,—its fruition Paradise, its defeat perdition. But in Tolstoy, almost for the first time, we are shown that passion is merely a condition; and that it has almost nothing to do with happiness. Other novelists represent lovers as forced by their passion to an ecstasy of selfish joy, or an ecstasy of selfish misery; but he shows us that they are only the more bound by it to the rest of the world. It is in fact, so far as it eventuates in marriage, the beginning of subjection to humanity, and nothing in it concerns the lovers alone.

It is not the less but the more mystical for this; and Tolstoy does full justice to all its mystical beauty, its mystical power. Its power upon Natacha,—that pure, good, wise girl,—whom it suddenly blinds and bewilders till she must be saved from ruin in spite of herself, and almost by violence; and upon Anna Karénina,—that loving mother, true friend, and obedient wife,—are illustrated with a vividness which I know not where to match. Dolly's wretchedness with her faithless husband, Kitty's happiness in the constancy of Levine, are neither unalloyed; and in all the instances and examples of passion, we are aware of the author's sense of its merely provisional character. This appears perhaps most impressively in the scenes of Prince Andreí Bolkonsky's long dying, where Natacha, when restored and forgiven for her aberration, becomes as little to him at last as if she had succeeded in giving herself to Anatol Kuragin. The theory of such matters is, that the passion which unites them in life must bring them closer still in death; but we are shown that it is not so.

Passion, we have to learn from the great master, who here as everywhere humbles himself to the truth, has in it life and death; but of itself it is something only as a condition precedent to these: without it neither can be; but it is lost in their importance, and is strictly subordinate to their laws. It has never been more charmingly and reverently studied in its beautiful and noble phases than it is in Tolstoy's fiction; though he has always dealt with it so sincerely, so seriously. As to its obscure and ugly and selfish phases, he is so far above all others who have written of it, that he alone seems truly to have divined it, or portrayed it as experience knows it. He never tries to lift it out of nature in either case, but leaves it more visibly and palpably a part of the lowest as well as the highest humanity.

He is apt to study both aspects of it in relation to death; so apt that I had almost said he is fond of doing it. He often does this in "War and Peace"; and in "Anna Karénina" the unity of passion and death might be said to be the principle and argument of the story. In "The Death of Ivan Ilyitch" the unworthy passion of the marriage is a part of the spiritual squalor in which the wretched worldling goes down to his grave. In the "Kreutzer Sonata" it is the very essence of the murder; and in the "Powers of Darkness" it is the spring of the blackest evil. I suppose that one thing which has made Tolstoy most distasteful to man-made society is, that in all sins from passion he holds men chiefly accountable. It is their luxury which is so much to blame for the perversion. I can recall, at the moment, only one woman—the Princess Helena—in whom he censures the same evils; and even in her he lets you feel that her evil is almost passive, and such as man-made society chiefly forced upon her. Tolstoy has always done justice to women's nature; he has nowhere mocked or satirized them without some touch of pity or extenuation: and he brings Anna Karénina through her passion to her death, with that tender lenity for her sex which recognizes womanhood as indestructibly pure and good.

He comes nearer unriddling life for us than any other writer. He persuades us that it cannot possibly give us any personal happiness; that there is no room for the selfish joy of any one except as it displaces the joy of some other, but that for unselfish joy there is infinite place and occasion. With the same key he unlocks the mystery of death; and he imagines so strenuously that death is neither more nor less than a transport of self-surrender, that he convinces the reason where there can be no proof. The reader will not have forgotten how in those last moments of earth which he has depicted, it is this utter giving up which is made to appear the first moment of heaven. Nothing in his mastery is so wonderful as his power upon us in the scenes of the borderland where his vision seems to pierce the confines of another world. He comes again and again to it, as if this exercise of his seership had for him the same fascination that we feel in it: the closing hours of Prince Andreí, the last sorrowful instants of Anna Karénina, the triumphal abnegation of the philistine Ivan Ilyitch, the illusions and disillusions of the dying soldier in "Scenes of the Siege of Sebastopol," the transport of the sordid merchant giving his life for his servant's in "Master and Man,"—all these, with perhaps others that fail to occur to me, are qualified by the same conviction, imparting itself so strongly that it is like a proven fact.

Of a man who can be so great in the treatment of great things, we can ask ourselves only after a certain reflection whether he is as great as some lesser men in some lesser things; and I have a certain diffidence in inquiring whether Tolstoy is a humorist. But I incline to think that he is, though the humor of his facts seeks him rather than he it. One who feels life so keenly cannot help feeling its grotesqueness through its perversions, or help smiling at it, with whatever pang in his heart. I should say that his books rather abounded in characters helplessly comic. Oblensky in "Anna Karénina," the futile and amiably unworthy husband of Dolly, is delicious; and in "War and Peace," old Count Rostof, perpetually insolvent, is pathetically ridiculous,—as Levine in the first novel often is, and Pierre Bezukhof often is in the second. His irony, without harshness or unkindness, often pursues human nature in its vain twistings and turnings, with effects equally fresh and true; as where Nikolai Rostof, flying before the French, whom he had just been trying his worst to kill, finds it incredible that they should be seeking to harm one whom he knew to be so kind and good as himself. In Polikoushka, where the two *muzhiks* watching by the peasant's dead body try to shrink into themselves when some polite people come in, and to make themselves small because they are aware of smelling of the barn-yard, there is the play of such humor as we find only now and then in the supreme humorists. As for pathos, the supposed corollary of humor, I felt that I had scarcely known what it might be till I read Tolstoy. In literature, so far as I know it, there is nothing to match with the passage describing Anna Karénina's stolen visit to her little son after she has deserted her husband.

I touch this instance and that, in illustration of one thing and another; but I feel after all as if I had touched almost nothing in Tolstoy, so much remains untouched; though I am aware that I should have some such feeling if I multiplied the instances indefinitely. Much is said of the love of nature in writers, who are supposed to love it as they catalogue or celebrate its facts; but in Tolstoy's work the nature is there just as the human nature is: simple, naked, unconscious. There is the sky that is really over our heads; there is the green earth, the open air; the seasons come and go: it is all actual, palpable,—and the joy of it as uncontrived apparently as the story which it environs, and which gives no more the sense of invention than the history of some veritable passage of human events. In "War and Peace" the fortunes of the fictitious personages are treated in precisely the same spirit, and in the same manner, as the fortunes of the real personages: Bezukhof and Napoleon are alike real.

Of methods in Tolstoy, then, there can scarcely be any talk. He has apparently no method: he has no purpose but to get what he thinks, simply and clearly before us. Of style there seems as little to say; though here, since I know him only in translation, I cannot speak confidently. He may have a very marked style in Russian; but if this was so, I do not see how it could be kept out of the versions. In any case, it is only when you come to ask yourself what it is, that you realize its absence. His books are full of Tolstoy,—his conviction, his experience,—and yet he does not impart his personal quality to the diction as other masters do. It would indeed be as hard to

imitate the literature as the life of Tolstoy, which will probably find only a millennial succession.

PART II: AMERICAN WRITERS

Introduction

Nine years after the appearance of *Criticism and Fiction* in 1891, Howells published another collection of critical essays, *Literary Friends and Acquaintance, A Personal Retrospect of American Authorship*. In this delightful book we walk the shaded streets of Cambridge with the youthful Howells, share his trepidation at conversing with Lowell in his study, visit Hawthorne and Emerson with him in Concord. There is no "sound of battle" in these quiet, faintly humorous chapters on the early encounter of the young poet-reporter from the Middle West with literary deities of Boston, Cambridge, and Concord. Yet one feels between the lines the importance of this trip to New England not only because Howells was in a deep sense nourished on the American tradition, nor because Howells "thought it a favorable moment to propose himself as the assistant editor of the *Atlantic Monthly*," but also because the journey gave him "the intimacy of the New England country" as he could have had it in no other way. Howells not only sat at the feet of the writers he had been reading in his lonely Ohio days, but he also steeped his soul in "the summer sweetness" of old farmhouses, gray stone walls, orchards, and "thick-brackened valleys." But all this retrospective reappraisal of writers and countryside that charms the reader of *Literary Friends and Acquaintance*, this personal account of a sensitive young writer in the studies, drawing rooms, and offices of an established literary circle, we cannot, for want of space, include in our selections below.

We have chosen, instead, as the opening essay for Part II,* "Recollections of an Atlantic Editorship," written by Howells in 1907, when he was seventy years of age. Here with extraordinary accuracy he recalls the scenes of almost fifty years earlier, the personalities of former editors and contributors, the names of writers now forgotten, the literary and business customs of the *Atlantic Monthly*—then "in some sort a critical

* The notes to Part II begin on p. 219.

authority in a country where criticism is rare." This essay is the autobiography of an editor, eagerly following the realistic movement in Europe and personally welcoming young writers from remote parts of the United States. By thus encouraging talent from all corners of the country, Howells extended the borders of our national literature beyond the confines of New England. "The fact is," he observed, "we were growing, whether we liked it or not, more and more American. Without ceasing to be New England, without ceasing to be Bostonian, at heart, we had become southern, mid-western and far-western in our sympathies." With one eye on European novelists, whom he constantly reviewed, Howells was scanning the horizon for signs of "regionalism" in his own country. Henry James, weighing the merits of Europe and America as habitats for writers, recognized Howells' shrewd insight as an editor in encouraging all hopeful signs of the American novel, which, James pointed out, "had its first seeds . . . sown very exactly in Atlantic soil, . . . where Howells soon began editorially to cultivate them."

"Recollections" is followed by Howells' reviews of books by some of his contemporaries—such as John W. De Forest, Mark Twain, Edward Eggleston—whose reputations Howells' early reviews in the *Atlantic* helped to establish. For the most part, the reviews chosen reflect Howells' initial contact with unestablished writers, rather than his later, more "literary" appraisals of these authors, because these brief essays prove that Howells was a critic and editor of extraordinary acumen, boldness, and generosity. Furthermore, they make it evident that Howells knew from the beginning what he wanted of a writer—an honest reflection of the life of our country, whether it were "commonplace," or as in the case of James, "romantic," in a very special sense. The lesson Howells was learning from Europe—that the truly observed carries its own sufficient beauty—he taught by example and precept to the American writers of his day. This lesson was to Howells the meaning of realism.

The implications of this much-discussed word realism are suggested in an essay "William Dean Howells," by Thomas Sergeant Perry, published in the *Century Magazine* of March, 1882, several months before Howells resigned from the

Atlantic and sailed for Europe. Perry understood that what Howells had attempted as a contributor to the magazine threw light on what he had been seeking as its editor. *A Chance Acquaintance, The Lady of the Aroostook,* and *Dr. Breen's Practice* were to this critic not merely pleasant diversions; they reflected an important break with the English novel, directing the way to the sort of fiction that catches "a truly national spirit." Wrote Perry:

> In so many formless English novels we see the frank acceptance of conventional rewards, the bride and the money-bags awaiting the young man who has artificially prolonged a tepid courtship, that the reader grows weary of the implied compliment to wealth and position. There is a truly national spirit in the way Mr. Howells shows the other side—the emptiness of convention and the dignity of native worth. . . . After all, what can realism produce but the downfall of conventionality? Just as the scientific spirit digs the ground from beneath superstition, so does its fellow worker, realism, tend to prick the bubble of abstract types. Realism is the tool of the democratic spirit, the modern spirit, by means of which the truth is elicited, and Mr. Howell's realism is tireless. It is, too, unceasingly good-natured. . . . We feel that Mr. Howells is scrutinizing the person he is writing about with undisturbed calmness, and that no name and no person can impose upon him by its conventional value.

The concept of realism, as an aspect of the modern spirit, is essentially the interpretation Howells enlarged upon in "The Editor's Study." The reviews written for *Harper's* merely indicate how in the 1880's and 1890's Howells' understanding of the term was deepened by the circumstances of his life in New York, where he came into contact with a larger, more cosmopolitan circle of men and women.

Howells and the Atlantic

In the *Atlantic Monthly* of November, 1907, W. D. Howells, the third editor of that magazine, wrote the memoirs of his editorship to celebrate the fiftieth birthday of a publication that had occupied a unique position in the cultural pattern of this country. Howells' "Recollections of an Atlantic Editorship" is not only a mine of information on the publishing conditions of a hundred years ago and a roll call of writers of the day, but it is also the most intimate picture we have of Howells functioning in the Tremont Street office of the *Atlantic* in his dual capacity of editor and contributor to its pages. What other editor ever corrected so painstakingly both manuscript and proof; who but Howells ever welcomed so cordially literary aspirants from all parts of the country; who but he ever formed so many permanent friendships from such an extraordinary variety of contacts? The fact that Howells himself was moving rapidly through his apprentice years as a novelist at the same time that he was establishing himself as an editor made all the difference in the critical and personal advice he gave to writers. For he was a fellow craftsman, venturing into the new and wide-open field of realistic fiction, a field so rich and promising that he generously encouraged others to follow. The names of some of those who accepted the invitation are found in the headings of the reviews below; the "Recollections of an Atlantic Editorship" lists dozens more, of lesser fame today, who in their way contributed to what soon became a movement of enormous importance in American culture. The meaning of realism, which Howells learned in part through his "European Masters," he translated into native terms, and as editor of the *Atlantic,* he interpreted these ideas to his readers through publication of the work of unknown young American writers.

Literary Friends and Acquaintance tells how Howells, recently returned from a consulship in Venice and not yet thirty years old, became in 1866 assistant to James T. Fields, then editor of the *Atlantic*. In those pages, too, one goes back still farther and participates in the dinner at the Parker House, when Howells made his famous pilgrimage to Boston in 1860. At that time the first editor of the *Atlantic,* James Russell Lowell, together with James T. Fields, the second editor, and Oliver Wendell Holmes, accepted the young Ohioan into their charmed circle, partly on the strength of several poems published in the *Atlantic,* but more especially because of the winning personality of this entirely literary young man of twenty-three, who carried with him a peculiar air of determination. Before the meal was over Holmes turned to Lowell, with the laughing remark, "Well, James, this is something like the apostolic succession; this is the laying on of hands."

In his "Recollections" at the age of seventy, Howells continued the story begun in *Literary Friends and Acquaintance,* from the moment of the official parting with his "kindly chief," James T. Fields, and his assumption of the editorship of the *Atlantic* in 1871. Howells tells us modestly: "The magazine was already established in its traditions when I came to it, and when I left it fifteen years later it seemed to me that if I had done any good it was little more than to fix it more firmly in them." A reading of the "Recollections" and the volumes of the *Atlantic* during this period convinces one that Howells, in fact, slowly and tactfully extended the confines of this New England publication. When he says, "To the reviews of American and English books I added certain pages of notices of French and German literature," we realize that by doing so, the new editor thereby placed the magazine in the stream of European thought, where realism was already a strong movement. When Howells tells us that he himself "read all the manuscripts which claimed critical attention," that he personally and in longhand "wrote to contributors who merited more than a printed circular," we realize that this tireless editor was actually sowing the seeds of the new movement in this country. When we are told further that Howells "was writing not only criticism, but sketches, stories, and poems for the body of the magazine, and, in the course of time, a novel each year," we are convinced that the third editor of the *Atlantic* did indeed lay the basis of the magazine that in 1957 marked its centennial. "I found it by no means drudgery," said Howells, referring to his long hours in the Tremont Street office; he admitted, however, that he never liked writing criticism and never satisfied himself in his reviews. His increasing occupation with fiction left him too little time for the book notices for the magazine, and these he turned over to younger men.

Howells' welcome to Miss Murfree, Miss Sarah Orne Jewett, Bret Harte, S. Weir Mitchell, described below, is typical of the cordial reception he accorded many authors now almost forgotten. Would that we could rummage with Howells in "that half-barrel of accepted manuscripts" that came down to him from his predecessors, Lowell and Fields; Howells passed on to the next editor, Thomas Bailey Aldrich, "a half-peck" of these yellowing sheets, and Aldrich promptly returned them to their authors. So busy was Howells with his "fictioning," he tells us, that he kept many "a poor contributor" of "the patient tribe" waiting at his door, his unread manuscript lying in one of "the darkling drawers" of his desk, while the harassed young editor polished off his own contribution. Howells' double role of editor and contributor proved finally too much even for his energy, and ill health forced him to resign from the *Atlantic* in 1881. After some time spent in European travel, he returned to the United States and in 1885 signed a contract with Harper's, the publishing house with which he remained, with a brief interruption, until his death.

From the offices of various publications of Harper's, Howells' "open editorial hand" was extended from 1886 to 1920, with unflagging cordiality, to the promising young writers who joined forces with him in what Stephen Crane called "the beautiful war" for truth in literature. Howells greeted Frank Norris as a new recruit in the battle; the younger novelist, under the influence of Zola, was transforming realism into something called "naturalism," a term not new to Howells.

Norris' thinly disguised portrait of Howells in "The Lost Story," quoted below, is a reminder of how the younger generation (Norris was an infant when Howells became editor of the *Atlantic* in 1871, and Crane was born late in the same year) regarded the short, stocky "Dean of American Literature" at the turn of the century. His stamp of approval was "sterling"; his style seemed by 1900 somewhat tame. He was, Norris tells us:

> . . . a short, rotund man, rubicund as to face, bourgeois as to clothes and surroundings . . . jovial in manner, indulging even in slang. One might easily set him down as a retired groceryman—wholesale, perhaps, but none the less a groceryman. Yet touch him upon the subject of his profession, and the *bonhomie* lapsed away from him at once. . . . Then he became serious. . . . This elderly man of letters, who had seen the rise and fall of a dozen schools, was above the influence of fads, and he whose books were among the classics even before his death, was infallible in his judgments on the work of the younger writers. All the stages of their evolution were known to him—all their mistakes, all their successes. He understood; and a story by one of them, a poem, a novel, that bore the stamp of his approval, was "sterling."

"Bourgeois" though Howells appeared to the young Norris, recently returned from a year in Paris, one must also observe that "in his judgment of the works of the younger writers," the occupant of "The Easy Chair" seemed to one of them "infallible." But more arresting to the "new critics" of Norris' day than his words of appreciation was the image of "a retired groceryman" caught by his pen. Soon Gertrude Atherton was asking in the *North American Review*, May, 1904, pointing her finger at Howells: "Why is American Literature Bourgeois?" Since this "elderly man of letters" had, as Norris observed, "seen the rise and fall of a dozen schools," he happily disregarded his detractors when he compiled "The Recollections of an Atlantic Editorship" three years later.

RECOLLECTIONS OF AN ATLANTIC EDITORSHIP*

In another place I have told how I came to be the assistant of Mr. Fields in the editorship of the Atlantic Monthly. That

was in 1866, and in 1872[1] he gave up to me the control
which he had held rather more in form than in fact from the
time I joined him. He had left the reading of manuscripts to
me, and almost always approved my choice in them, only re-
serving to himself the supreme right of accepting things I had
not seen, and of inviting contributions. It was a suzerainty
rather than a sovereignty which he exercised, and I might well
have fancied myself independent under it. I never thought of
questioning his easy over-lordship, and my assistant editorship ended with far more regret to me than my editorship,
when in 1881 I resigned it to Mr. Aldrich.

I recall very distinctly the official parting with my kindly
chief in his little room looking into the corner of the Common
at 124 Tremont Street, for it was impressed upon me by
something that had its pathos then, and has it now. In the
emotion I felt at his willingness to give up his high place (it
seemed to me one of the highest), I asked him why he wished
to do it, with a wonder at which he smiled from his fifty-six
years down upon my thirty-five. He answered, what I very
well knew, that he was tired of it, and wanted time and a
free mind to do some literary work of his own. "Besides," he
added, with a cheerfulness that not only touched but dismayed
me, "I think people generally have some foreknowledge of
their going; I am past fifty, and I do not expect to live long."
He did not cease smiling as he said this, and I cannot recall
that in my amaze I answered with any of the usual protests
we make against the expression of far less frank and open pre-
science. He lived much longer than he expected, after he had
felt himself a stricken man; but still it was not many years before he died, when a relation marred by scarcely a moment
of displeasure, and certainly without one unkindness from
him, had altogether ceased.

The magazine was already established in its traditions when
I came to it, and when I left it fifteen years later it seemed to
me that if I had done any good it was little more than to fix
it more firmly in them. During the nine years of its existence
before my time it had the best that the greatest writers of
New England could give it. First of these were, of course,

Longfellow, Emerson, Hawthorne, Whittier, Holmes, Lowell, Mrs. Stowe, and Bryant, and after them followed a long line of gifted people, whom but to number will recall many names of the second brilliancy, with some faded or fading beyond recall. I will not attempt a full list, but my memories of the Atlantic would be very faulty if they did not include the excellence in verse or prose of such favorites[2] as Agassiz, Mrs. Paul Akers, Mr. Alden, Aldrich, Boker, Mr. Burroughs, Alice Cary, Caroline Chesebro', Lydia Maria Child, James Freeman Clarke, Conway, Rose Terry Cooke, Cranch, Curtis, J. W. De Forest, Mrs. Diaz, Rebecca Harding Davis, Mrs. Fields, J. T. Fields, Henry Giles, Annie Douglas Greene, Dr. E. E. Hale, Lucretia Hale, Gail Hamilton, Colonel Higginson, G. S. Hillard, J. G. Holland, Mrs. Howe, Henry James, father and son, Lucy Larcom, Fitz Hugh Ludlow, Donald G. Mitchell, Walter Mitchell, Fitz-James O'Brien, J. W. Palmer, Francis Parkman, T. W. Parsons, Norah Perry, Mr. and Mrs. J. J. Piatt, Buchanan Read, Epes Sargent, Mrs. Prescott Spofford, W. J. Stillman, R. H. Stoddard, Elizabeth Stoddard, W. W. Story, Bayard Taylor, Celia Thaxter, Thoreau, Mr. J. T. Trowbridge, Mrs. Stuart Phelps Ward, David A. Wasson, E. P. Whipple, Richard Grant White, Adeline D. T. Whitney, Forceythe Wilson, Theodore Winthrop.

The .tale is very long, but it might be lengthened a third without naming other names which could accuse me of having forgotten many delightful authors remembered by my older readers, and in some instances known to my younger readers. In the alphabetical course there is here no intimation of the writers' respective order or degree, and their quantity is as little suggested. Many of them were frequent contributors of very even excellence; others wrote one thing, or one or two or three things, that caught the public fancy with as potent appeal as the best of the many things that others did. Some of those who were conspicuous in 1866 lost their foremost place, and others then of no wider celebrity grew in fame that would rank them with those greatest ones whom I have mentioned first.

Beginning myself to contribute to the magazine in its third year, I held all its contributors in a devout regard and did not presume to distinguish between the larger and lesser luminaries, though I knew very well which I liked best. I was one of four singularly favored youths beyond the Alleghanies who suffered more than once in the company of those gods and half-gods and quarter-gods of New England; the other two lonely Westerners I met in those gleaming halls of morn being my room-mate in Columbus, A. T. Fullerton, and another, my friend and fellow-poet Piatt in Louisville. Leonard Case[3] dwelt in a lettered and moneyed seclusion (as we heard) at Cleveland, but Alice Cary had lived so long in the East that she was less an Ohioan than one of those few New Yorkers admitted with the overwhelming majority of New Englanders, whom I figured standing aloof from all us outsiders.

It was with a sort of incredulous gasping that I realized myself in authority with these when it came to that, and I should not now be able to say how or why it came to that, without allowing merits in myself which I should be the last to assert. These things are always much better attributed to Fortune, or at the furthest to Providence. What I know is that it was wonderful to me to go through the editorial record (which with my want of method I presently disused) and find my own name among the Accepted and the Rejected. It was far oftenest among the rejected; but there was a keener pleasure in those rejections, which could not now be repeated, than in the acceptances which stretched indefinitely before me.

Otherwise the record, where the disappointments so heavily outnumbered the fruitions, had its pathos; and at first I could not return a manuscript without a pang. But in a surprisingly little time that melting mood congealed into an icy indifference, if it did not pass into the sort of inhuman complacency of the judge who sentences a series of proven offenders. We are so made that we quickly turn the enemies of those who give us trouble; the hunter feels himself the foe of the game that leads him a long and difficult chase; and in like manner the editor wreaks a sort of revenge in rejecting the contributor who has bothered him to read a manuscript quite through before it yields itself unfit for publication. Perhaps I am painting the case in rather blacker colors than the fact would justify, though there is truth in what I say. Yet, for the most part, the affair did not come to this. It was at first surprising, and when no longer surprising it was gratifying, to find that the vast mass of the contributions fixed their own fate, almost at a glance. They were of subjects treated before, or subjects not to be treated at all, or they were self-condemned by their uncouth and slovenly style, or were written in a hand so crude and ignorant that it was at once apparent that they had not the root of literature in them. The hardest of all to manage were those which had some savor of acceptance in them; which had promise, or which failed so near the point of success that it was a real grief to refuse them. Conscience then laid it upon me to write to the authors and give hopes, or reasons, or tender excuses, and not dismiss any of them with the printed circular that carried insult and despair in the smooth uncandor of its assurance that the contribution in question was not declined necessarily because of a want of merit in it.

The poor fellows, and still more the poor dears, were apt in the means by which they tried to find a royal road to the public through the magazine. Claims of acquaintance with friends of the editors, distressful domestic circumstances, adverse fortune, irresistible impulse to literature, mortal sickness in which the last hours of the writer would be brightened by seeing the poem or story in print, were the commonest appeals. These must have been much alike, or else I should remember more distinctive cases. One which I do remember was that of a woman in the West who sent the manuscript of a serial story with a letter, very simply and touchingly confiding that in her youth she had an ardent longing to be an author. She had married, instead, and now at fifty, with her large family of children grown up about her, prosperous and happy, she felt again the impulse of her girlhood. She enclosed a ten-dollar note to pay the editor for the trouble of reading her story, and she wished his true opinion of it. I should have been hard-hearted indeed if I had not answered this letter at length, with a carefully considered criticism which I sincerely grieved that I could not make favorable, and returned the sum of my hire with every good wish. I could not feel it a bribe, and I could not quite believe that it was with the design of corrupting me, that a very unliterary author came one day with two dollars to pay me for noticing his book. He said he had been told that this was the way to get it noticed.

In those days, and for seven or eight years afterwards, I wrote nearly all the "Literary Notices" in the magazine. When I began to share the work with others, and at last to leave it almost wholly to them, they and I wrote so very much alike that I could not always be sure which notices I had done. That is a very common psychological event in journalism, when one prevalent will has fixed the tone, and I was willful, if not strong, in my direction after I came into full control. I never liked writing criticism, and never pleased myself in it; but I should probably have kept writing most of the Atlantic notices to the end, if my increasing occupation with fiction had not left me too few hours out of the twenty-four for them. The editorial salary I received covered the pay for my contributions, but I represented to the publishers that I could not write everything in the magazine, and they saw the reason of my delegating the notices. I had the help of the best young critics whom I knew, and who abounded in Boston and Cambridge; and after I succeeded Mr. Fields, I enlarged the editorial departments at the end of the magazine so as to include comment on politics, art, and music, as well as literature. For a while, I think for a year, I indulged the fancy of printing each month a piece of original music, with original songs; but though both the music and the songs were good, or at least from our best younger composers and poets, the feature did not please,—I do not know why,—and it was presently omitted.

To the reviews of American and English books I added certain pages of notices of French and German literature, and in these I had the very efficient and singularly instructed help of Mr. Thomas Sergeant Perry, who knew not only more of current continental literature than any other American, but more than all the other Americans. He wrote cleverly and facilely, and I felt that his work had unique value too little recognized by the public, and to which I should feel it a duty, if it were not so entirely a pleasure, to bear witness here. He was one of the many new contributors with whom I had the good fortune to work forward in the magazine. I could not exaggerate his rare qualifications for the work he undertook; his taste, and his temperament, at once just and humane, were equal to his unrivaled knowledge. It is not too much to say that literally he read every important French and German book which appeared, not only in fiction, but in history, biography, criticism, and metaphysics, as well as those exact sciences which are nearest allied to the humanities.

I grouped the books according to their kinds, in the critical department, but eventually I broke from the departmental form altogether, and began to print the different groups and the longer reviews as separate articles. It was a way of adding to the apparent as well as real variety of the table of contents which has approved itself to succeeding editors.

In the course of time, but a very long time, the magazine felt the need of a more informal expression than it found in the stated articles, and the Contributors' Club took the place of all the different departments, those of politics, music, and art having been dropped before that of literature. The new idea was talked over with the late George Parsons Lathrop, who had become my assistant, and we found no way to realize it but by writing the first paragraphs ourselves, and so tempting others to write for the Club. In the course of a very few months we had more than help enough, and could easily drop out of the coöperation.

Except for the brief period of a year or eighteen months, I had no assistance during my editorship. During the greater part of the time I had clerkly help, most efficient, most intelligent; but I read all the manuscripts which claimed critical attention; I wrote to contributors who merited more than a printed circular; I revised all the proofs, verifying every quotation and foreign word, and correcting slovenly style and syntax, and then I revised the author's and my own corrections. Meantime I was writing not only criticisms, but sketches, stories, and poems for the body of the magazine; and in the course of time, a novel each year. It seems like rather full work, but I had always leisure, and I made a long summer away from Cambridge in the country. The secret, if there was any secret, lay in my doing every day two or three hours' work, and letting no day pass idly. The work of reading manuscripts and writing letters could be pushed into a corner,

and taken out for some interval of larger leisure; and this
happened oftener and oftener as I grew more and more a
novelist, and needed every morning for fiction. The proof-
reading, which was seldom other than a pleasure, with its
tasks of revision and research, I kept for the later afternoons
and evenings; though sometimes it well-nigh took the character of original work, in that liberal Atlantic tradition of bet-
tering the authors by editorial transposition and paraphrase,
either in the form of suggestion or of absolute correction.
This proof-reading was a school of verbal exactness and rhe-
torical simplicity and clearness, and in it I had succeeded
others, my superiors, who were without their equals. It is still
my belief that the best proof-reading in the world is done in
Cambridge, Massachusetts, and it is probably none the worse
for my having a part in it no longer.

As I have intimated, I found it by no means drudgery;
though as for drudgery, I think that this is for the most part in
the doer of it, and it is always a very wholesome thing, even
when it is real, objective drudgery. It would be a much de-
center, honester, and juster world if we each took his share of
it, and I base my best hopes of the future in some such even-
tuality. Not only the proofs were a pleasing and profitable
drudgery, but the poor manuscripts, except in the most for-
bidding and hopeless instances, yielded their little crumbs of
comfort; they supported while they fatigued. Very often they
startled the drooping intelligence with something good and
new amidst their impossibility; very often, when they treated
of some serious matter, some strange theme, some unvisited
country, some question of unimagined import, they instructed and delighted the judge who knew himself inexorably
averse to their acceptance, for editorial reasons; they, condemned to darkness and oblivion, enlightened and edified
him with some indelible thought, some fresh, or some freshly
related, fact. My information is not of so great density yet but
I can still distinguish points in its nebulous mass, from time to
time, which I cannot follow to their luminous source in the
chapter or verse of any book I have read. These, I suspect,
derive from some far-forgotten source in the thousands of
manuscripts which in my fifteen editorial years I read and rejected.

The rejection of a manuscript often left a pang, but the acceptable manuscript, especially from an unknown hand, brought a glow of joy which richly compensated me for all I suffered from the others.[4] To feel the touch never felt before, to be the first to find the planet unimagined in the illimitable heaven of art, to be in at the dawn of a new talent, with the light that seems to mantle the written page: who would not be an editor, for such a privilege? I do not know how it is with other editors who are also authors, but I can truly say for myself that nothing of my own which I thought fresh and true ever gave me more pleasure than that I got from the like qualities in the work of some young writer revealing his power.

It was quite as often *her* power, for in our beloved republic of letters the citizenship is not reserved solely to males of twenty-one and over. I have not counted up the writers who came forward in these pages during my time, and I do not know which sex prevails in their number, but if any one were to prove that there were more women than men, I should not be surprised. I do not remember any man who feigned himself a woman, but now and then a woman liked to masquerade as a man, though the disguise never deceived the editor, even when it deceived the reader, except in the very signal and very noted instance of Miss Mary N. Murfree, whom, till I met her face to face, I never suspected for any but Charles Egbert Craddock. The severely simple, the robust, the athletic, hand which she wrote would have sufficed to carry conviction of her manhood against any doubt. But I had no doubts. I believe I took the first story she sent, and for three or four years I addressed my letters of acceptance, or criticism, to Charles Egbert Craddock, Murfreesboro', Tennessee, without the slightest misgiving. Then she came to Boston, and Aldrich, who had succeeded me, and who had already suffered the disillusion awaiting me, asked me to meet Craddock at dinner. He had asked Dr. Holmes and Lawrence Barrett, too; and I should not attempt to say whose astonishment he enjoyed most. But I wish I could recall word for word the exquisite terms in which Dr. Holmes turned his discomfiture into triumph in that most delicately feminine presence.

The proof of identity, if any were needed, came with the

rich, full pipe of a voice in which she answered our words and gasps of amaze. In literary history I fancy there has been no such perfect masquerade; but masquerade was the least part of Miss Murfree's success. There seems in the dust and smoke of the recent literary explosions an eclipse of that fine talent, as strong as it is fine, and as native as it is rare; but I hope that when the vaporous reputations blow away, her clear light will show the stronger for its momentary obscuration. She was the first to express a true Southern quality in fiction, and it was not the less Southern because it rendered the strange, rude, wild life of a small section of the greater section which still unhappily remains a section. One might have said, looking back from the acknowledged fact of her personality, that a woman of the Rosa Bonheur type could well have caught the look of that half-savagery in her men; but that only a man could have touched in the wilding, flower-like, pathetic loveliness of the sort of heroine she gave to art.

She was far from the first, and by no means the last of those women, not less dear than great, whose work carried forward the early traditions of studied beauty in the magazine with something newer and racier in the flavor and fragrance of their fiction. I must name at the head of these that immediate classic Miss Sarah Orne Jewett, whose incomparable sketches of New England character began to appear well within my assistant-editorship, with whatever credit to me I may not rob my chief of. The truth is, probably, that he liked them as well as I, and it was merely my good luck to be the means of encouraging them in the free movement, unfettered by the limits of plot, and keeping only to the reality, which no other eye than hers has seen so subtly, so humorously, so touchingly. It is the foible of editors, if it is not rather their forte, to flatter themselves that though they may not have invented their contributions, they have at least invented their contributors; and if any long-memoried reader chooses to hail me an inspired genius because of my instant and constant appreciation of Miss Jewett's writing, I shall be the last to snub him down.

Without greatly fearing my frown, he may attribute a like merit to me for having so promptly and unremittingly recognized the unique artistry and beauty of Mr. Henry James's work. My desert in valuing him is so great that I can freely confess the fact that two of his stories and one of his criticisms appeared in the magazine some years before my time, though perhaps not with the band of music with which I welcomed every one afterwards. I do not know whether it was to try me on the story, or the story on me, that my dear chief (who was capable of either subtlety) gave me the fourth of Mr. James's contributions to read in the manuscript; but I was equal to either test, and returned it with the jubilant verdict, "Yes, and as many more as you can get from the author." He was then writing also for other magazines; after that I did my best to keep him for the Atlantic, and there was but one of his many and many contributions about which we differed.[5] This was promptly printed elsewhere; but though I remember it very well, I will not name it, for we might differ about it still, and I would not make the reader privy to a quarrel where all should be peace.

I feel a danger to the general peace in mentioning certain favorite contributors without mentioning others who have an equal right; but if it is understood that some are mentioned with a bad conscience for those passed in silence (I was not asked to write this whole number of the magazine) I hope I shall be forgiven. There was now and then a single contribution, or two contributions, which gave me high hopes of the author, but which were followed by no others, or no others so acceptable. Among such was "Captain Ben's Choice," a sketch of New England shore-character by Mrs. Frances L. Pratt, done with an authentic touch, and as finely and firmly as something of Miss Jewett's or Mrs. Wilkins Freeman's. There were two stories, the only ones sent me, by Mrs. Sarah Butler Wister,[6] which had a distinction in the handling, and a penetrating quality in the imagining, far beyond that of most of the stories I was editorially proud of. Other contributors who began in Atlantic air were acclimated in another. In one volume I printed four poems, which I thought and still think admirable, by Miss Edith Jones, who needs only to be named as Mrs. Edith Wharton to testify to that prophetic instinct in me which every editor likes to think himself endowed with; it does not matter if the prophecy fulfills itself a little circuitously.

My liking for Dr. Weir Mitchell and his work was a taste likewise inherited from my chief, though, strictly speaking, we began contributor and assistant editor together. From the first there was something equally attractive to me in his mystic, his realistic, and his scientific things, perhaps because they were all alike scientific. "The Case of George Dedlock" and "Was He Dead?" gave me a scarcely different delight from that I took in "The Autobiography of a Quack." I have since followed the writer far in other fields, especially where he made his poetic ventures, but I keep a steadfast preference for those earlier things of his; I do not pretend it is a reasoned preference.

In another place (there are now so many other places!) I have told of my pleasure in the acquaintance, which instantly became friendship, with Hjalmar Hjorth Boyesen and his poetry; whether he wrote it in verse or prose, it was always poetry. I need not dwell here upon that pleasure which his too early death has tinged with a lasting grief; but surely the reader who shared the first joy of his "Gunnar" with me, would not like me to leave it unnamed among these memories. That romance was from the rapture of his own Norse youth and the youth of the Norse literature then so richly and fully adolescent in Björnson, and Lie,[7] and Kielland,[8] and hardening to its sombre senescence in Ibsen. Boyesen never surpassed "Gunnar" in the idyllic charm which in him was never at odds with reality; but he went forward from it, irregularly enough, as a novelist and critic and poet, till he arrived at his farthest reach in "The Mammon of Unrighteousness," a great picture of the American life which he painted with a mastery few born to it have equaled, and fewer yet surpassed.

There was long a superstition, which each of the editors before me had tried to enlighten, that the Atlantic was unfriendly to all literature outside of Boston or New England, or at the farthest, New York or Philadelphia. The fact was that there was elsewhere little writing worth printing in it; but that little it had cordially welcomed. When the little became a good deal the welcome was not more cordial, for it could not have been; and in seeking a further expansion, I was only fol-

lowing the tradition of the magazine. I cannot claim that
there was anything original in my passion for the common,
for "the familiar and the low," which Emerson held the
strange and high.⁹ Lowell had the same passion for it in the
intervals of his "toryism of the nerves," and nobody could
have tasted its raciness with a keener gusto than my chief.
But perhaps it was my sense not only of the quaint, the comic, but of the ever-poetic in the common, that made it dear to
me. It was with a tingling delight that I hailed any verification
of my faith in it, and among the confirmations which I received there was none stronger than that in the "Adirondack
Sketches" of Mr. Philip [Philander] Deming. They were,
whether instinctively or consciously, in the right manner, and
of simplicity in motive, material, and imagination as fine as
something Norse, or Slavic, or Italian, or Spanish. No doubt,
"Lida Ann," "Lost," "John's Trial," and "Willie" are distinguishable among the multitude of ghosts that haunt the memory of elder readers, but would only come to trouble joy in
the younger sort, who delight in the human-nature fakirs of
our latter-day fiction. Surely, in some brighter and clearer
future, such dear, and true, and rare creatures of the sympathetic mind must have their welcome palingenesis for all.

Mr. Deming was only of the West which is as near Boston
as Albany, but as I have said, there were four trans-Allegha-
nian poets, who had penetrated to the mournful and misty Atlantic (as they had feared it) from their native lakes and rivers. Even in the sixth year of the magazine, Bret Harte of California had appeared in it; and others of the San Francisco
school, notably Charles Warren Stoddard, had won an easy
entrance after him. Where, indeed, would Mr. Stoddard have
been denied, if he had come with something so utterly fresh
and delicious as "A Prodigal in Tahiti"? Branches he bore of
that and many another enchanted stem, which won his literature my love, and keep it to this day, so that a tender indignation rises in my heart when I find it is not known to every
one. John Hay, so great in such different kinds, came also
with verse and fiction, studies of the West, and studies of the
lingering East in Spain as he found it in his "Castilian Days."
Later came Mark Twain, originally of Missouri, but then pro-

visionally of Hartford, and now ultimately of the Solar System, not to say the Universe. He came first with "A True Story," one of those noble pieces of humanity with which the South has atoned chiefly if not solely through him for all its despite to the negro. Then he came with other things, but preeminently with "Old Times on the Mississippi," which I hope I am not too fondly mistaken in thinking I suggested his writing for the magazine. "A True Story" was but three pages long, and I remember the anxiety with which the business side of the magazine tried to compute its pecuniary value. It was finally decided to give the author twenty dollars a page, a rate unexampled in our modest history. I believe Mr. Clemens has since been offered a thousand dollars a thousand words, but I have never regretted that we paid him so handsomely for his first contribution. I myself felt that we were throwing in the highest recognition of his writing as literature, along with a sum we could ill afford; but the late Mr. Houghton, who had then become owner and paymaster, had no such reflection to please him in the headlong outlay. He had always believed that Mark Twain was literature, and it was his zeal and courage which justified me in asking for more and more contributions from him, though at a lower rate. We counted largely on his popularity to increase our circulation when we began to print the piloting papers; but with one leading journal in New York republishing them as quickly as they appeared, and another in St. Louis supplying the demand of the Mississippi Valley, and another off in San Francisco offering them to his old public on the Pacific slope, the sales of the Atlantic Monthly were not advanced a single copy, so far as we could make out. Those were the simple days when the magazines did not guard their copyright as they do now; advance copies were sent to the great newspapers, which helped their readers to the plums, poetic and prosaic, before the magazine could reach the news-stands, and so relieved them of the necessity of buying it.

Among other contributors to whom we looked for prosperity and by whom we looked for prosperity and by whom we were disappointed of it, was Charles Reade, whose star has now declined so far that it is hard to believe that at the time

we printed his "Griffith Gaunt" it outshone or presently out-
flashed any other light of English fiction. We had also a short
serial story from Charles Dickens, eked out into three numbers for which we paid (I remember gasping at the monstrous sum) a thousand dollars; and one poem by Tennyson,
and several by Browning, without sensible pecuniary advantage. But this was in the earlier rather than the later part of
my term, that the transatlantic muse was more invited; I
thought either she did not give us of her best, or that she had
not anything so acceptable to give us as our own muse.

The fact is we were growing, whether we liked it or not,
more and more American. Without ceasing to be New England, without ceasing to be Bostonian, at heart, we had become southern, mid-western and far-western in our sympathies. It seemed to me that the new good things were coming
from those regions rather than from our own coasts and
hills, but it may have been that the things were newer oftener
than better. A careful count of heads might still show
that a majority of the good heads in the magazine were New
England heads. In my time, when I began to have it quite to
myself, our greatest writers continued to contribute, with the
seconding which was scarcely to be distinguished in quality.
As if from the grave, Hawthorne rose in the first number I
made up, with "Septimius Felton" in his wizard hand, amidst
a company of his living contemporaries who are mostly now
his fellow-ghosts. Dr. Holmes printed "The Poet at the Break-
fast-Table" in my earliest volumes, and thereafter with
touching fealty to the magazine responded to every appeal of
the young editor. Longfellow was constant, as before; Lowell
was even hurt when once, to spare him the tiresome repeti-
tion, I had not put his name in the prospectus; Emerson sent
some of his most Emersonian poems; Whittier was forgivingly
true to the flag, after its mistaken bearer had once refused
his following. Among the younger poets (I will call none of
them minor) Aldrich was as constant as Holmes, and Stedman as responsive as Longfellow; Bayard Taylor was generous of his best, as he had always been. Mrs. Stuart Phelps,
Mrs. Thaxter, Mrs. Prescott Spofford, Mrs. L. C. Moulton,
Mrs. Fields, Lucy Larcom, Mr. Trowbridge, wrote character-

istic verse which I cannot believe any one more valued than the new host who welcomed it.

If he welcomed from Indiana the note of Maurice Thompson with a glad sense of its freshness, he accepted every one of the twelve pieces offred him by Hiram Rich[10] of Gloucester, Massachusetts, with as deep a pleasure in their new touch; and he printed as eagerly the richly fancied, richly pictorial poems of that sadly unvalued true poet, Edgar Fawcett. Helen Hunt Jackson of Massachusetts and Paul H. Hayne of South Carolina had always the same hospitality if not always the same esteem. They were poets both, though one is scarcely more remembered than the other. Constance Fenimore Woolson of Cleveland sent stories and studies of life in the Great Lake lands; and Mr. William Henry Bishop[11] of Milwaukee contributed a romance which those who have not forgotten "Detmold" must remember for the restraint and delicacy with which a new motive in fiction was managed, and the truth with which the daring situation was imagined. George Parsons Lathrop, Hawaiian-born and German-bred, came to my help in the editorship about the time that the most American of Scotchmen, Robert Dale Owen, was writing his charming autobiography in separable chapters, after the fashion adopted by that most American of Englishmen, James Parton, in printing his biography of Jefferson. John Fiske, one of the most autochthonic of New Englanders, pursued at my suggestion the same method with the papers forming his "Myths and Myth-Makers,"[12] and began with them his long line of popular contributions to the magazine, though some minor articles had preceded them. Another New Englander, quite as autochthonic, began contributor with a series of brilliant sketches, and ended with a series of papers on "Sanitary Drainage" which were equally characteristic of his various talent. This was George E. Waring, who had been the soldier he always looked, and who had afterwards the boldness to dream of cleaning New York, and when he had realized his dream, went to Cuba and died a hero of humanity in the cause of sanitary science. Yet another New Englander of almost equal date, as absolutely New England in his difference from the others as either, was that gentle and fine and quaint Charles Dudley Warner; his studies of travel shed a light on these pages as from a clear lamp of knowledge, which every now and then emitted a flash of the tricksy gayety, the will-o'-the-wisp humor, pervading his playful essays.

It is in vain that I try to separate my editorial achievements from those of my immediate predecessor. I had certainly the indisputable credit of suggesting, if not instigating, the publication of Mrs. Frances Kemble's autobiography by asking why she did not write it, when I already knew she was writing it, and so perhaps taking her fancy. But shall I claim the honor of being Aldrich's editor, because I published all his romances and many of his best poems? Many others yet of his best had appeared in the Atlantic during my own literary nonage, when I classed him with Longfellow and Lowell in his precocious majority; and the reader may be sure there were none of his pieces in that half-barrel of accepted manuscripts which came down to me from the first as well as the second editor of the magazine.

I say half-barrel, but if that seems too much I will compromise on a bushel, on condition that it shall be full measure, pressed down and running over. From the beginning up to my time and all through it, the custom of the magazine had been to pay for contributions on publication, and such inhibition as fear of the publisher's check had not been laid upon Lowell's literary tenderness or Fields's generous hopefulness when it came to the question of keeping some passable sketch, or article, or story, or poem. These were now there, in all their sad variety, in that half-barrel, or call it bushel, which loomed a hogshead in my view, when my chief left it to me. But I was young and strong, and comparatively bold, and I grappled with these manuscripts at once. I will not pretend that I read them; for me the fact that they were accepted was enough, if they still had any life in them. The test was very simple. If the author was still living, then his contribution was alive; if he was dead, then it was dead too; and I will never confess with what ghoulish glee I exulted in finding a manuscript exanimate. With the living I struggled through a long half-score of years, printing them as I could, and if any author dropped by the way, laying his unpublished manuscript like a laurel crown upon his tomb. When Aldrich came to my relief, I placed a pathetic remnant of the bushel, say a half-peck, in his hands, and it was with a shock that I learned later of his acting upon a wholly different conception of his duty to these heirlooms; he sent them all back, dead or alive, and so made an end of an intolerable burden.

I do not blame him for this short and easy method with them; I am not sure but it would be well for mankind if we could use some such method with all the heirlooms of the past. But now that I am no longer an editor, and am without the reasonable hope of ever being one again, I am going to free my mind with regard to the sin I once shared. I think an editor has no right to accept a contribution unless he has some clear expectation of printing it within a reasonable time. His obligation toward the author is not discharged when he pays him; he is still bound to him in the debt of that publicity which the author was seeking from him and to which he has a right, as forming by far, especially if he is young and unknown, the greater part of his reward. In my time I was guilty of wrong in this sort to so many authors that if there is really going to be a Last Day I shall not know where to hide myself from them. In vain shall I plead a misplaced tenderness for their feelings; in vain a love for their work. I ought to have shielded them from both, and given them their contributions back with tears of praise, and hopes for them with other editors able to publish them soon, mingling with my fond regrets. Instead of that, I often kept them waiting a year, two years, three, five, when I had already kept them waiting months for a reading. The image of my desk is before me as I write, with unread manuscripts cumbering a corner of it, and I busy with my fictioning, and pretending that I was only seeking to get the mood and the moment together for reading them. These were selected manuscripts which I had dug out of darkling drawers where I had thrown them indiscriminately, good, bad, and indifferent, as they came, and now and then visited them, to satisfy my bad conscience, and pluck forth a possibility or two, and add it to the heap at the corner of my desk. There, if I had been as honest with myself as I am now trying to be with the reader, I should not have let them lie so long, how long! before I got the mood and moment together for them. That was a favorite phrase of mine, in those days; I remember using it with many contributors whom I cannot remember.

They are a patient tribe, these poor contributors, and they seldom turned upon me. Now and then they did, though, and wreaked a just resentment. This I took meekly when I had some excuse; when I had none, I returned it with a high professional scorn, tacit or explicit, which I am afraid editors still practice toward injured contributors; for if I, a very good man, as editors go, could carry myself so to their indignation, what must be the behavior of the average wicked editor of this degenerate day? I hate still to think of their vengeance, but how much more of their pardon, patient, silent, saintly?

But it was not to indulge these fond pleasures of autobiography that I began by speaking of the essential unity of editorial tradition. Fields had continued Lowell, and perforce I infrangibly continued Fields, coloring the web a little, it seems a very little, from my own tastes and opinions. Certain writers besides those I have already named wrote on from him to me. Prime among these was Harriet Beecher Stowe, and next her was our honored and revered Dr. Hale, whose charmingly ingenious work came to me first in "My Visit to Sybaris," and last in "Life in the Brick Moon": work not only charming and ingenious, but of a penetration, a presage, not yet fully realized through the play of humor and fancy. His peer and contemporary, Colonel Thomas Wentworth Higginson, who had written so much, and always in the interest of art and humanity, honored my page as he had that of my predecessors; but I came to my place too late to welcome a contemporary of both, the friend whom I cannot trust myself to praise except in naming him, Charles Eliot Norton. His scholarship, his taste, his skill were already dedicated to other tasks; he was, with Lowell, editor of the North American Review; and I never edited anything of his except one brief critical notice, though the tale of his earlier contributions to the magazine continued from the first number, in criticisms and essays, to the last number of Mr. Lowell's time. I was proud to edit the brilliant chapters which Francis Parkman continued to give the magazine from the forthcoming volumes of history, ranking him at the head of American

historians, and with the great historians of our time. The nat-
ural-historian, Mr. John Burroughs, who lives to instruct our
day in the modest and beautiful truth of the life so near and
yet so far from ours, was a guest of Fields's long before he
was mine; and Clarence King, worthy to be named with him
for the charm of his science, came distinctly within the time
of my suzerain. I read his proofs, though, and acclaimed the
literature which King was always humorously ready to dis-
claim. Among the first serials which I printed was that story
of Caroline Chesebro's, "The Foe in the Household," which I
still think of a singular excellence. Later, quite within my
time, were a novel and several short stories by William M.
Baker, so racy of the South, and so good of their kind, that I
remember them yet with satisfaction. Of the South, racy and
excellent too, were the "Rebel's Recollections" of Mr.
George Cary Eggleston, which it is pleasant to think that I
asked him to set down for the magazine. I have often testified my esteem for the novels of J. W. De Forest, which I was
so willing to print, and I need not repeat the witness here.
But I should wrong myself if I did not record my strong belief that I was among the first editors to recognize the admirable talent of Octave Thanet.

I should like to speak of them all, those contemporaries
and contributors of mine, whom naming a few of brings me
my old joy in, with a grief for leaving any unnamed. Their
successes could not have been dearer to them than they were
to me. As each new talent revealed itself to me I exulted in it
with a transport which I was sure the public would share with
me, and which, whether it fell out so or not, it was an unselfish
and unalloyed delight to edit, such as few things in life can
give. It was all very, very intimate, that relation of editor and
contributor. I do not mean as to personal acquaintance, for
in the vast, the overwhelming majority of cases, it never came
to that; but I mean the sort of metempsychosis by which I
was put so entirely in their place, became so more than one
with them, that any slight or wrong done them hurt me more
than if it were done to me. Each number of the magazine was
an ever new and ever dear surprise for me, at every advance
of its being, from the time I put it together in manuscript and
gave the copy to the printers until it came into my hands a

finished product from the bindery, smelling so intoxicatingly of the ink and paper. At the end of the editor's month, which was a full month before the reader's, there was a struggle with the physical limitations of the magazine which tasked all my powers. I went to have it out, first to the University Press, and then to the Riverside Press; and there I cut and hewed and pared at the quivering members of the closing pages till they came into bounds and the new number was ready to orb about in the space that was perhaps finally too large for it. For the publishers, the corrections, especially the excisions, were expensive pangs, like those of all surgery; but often I wished to avoid them by the yet more expensive enlargement of the magazine, entreating the publishers for eight pages more, or even for four, though I knew they must lose money by it.

There go with these more material memories flitting re-membrances, psychical to ineffability, of winter days, and laborious trudges to the printers' through the deep Cambridge snow, when the overwrought horse-car faltered in its track; and of Cambridge summer nights spent far toward their star-ry noons over obdurate proofs, while the crickets and the grasshoppers rasped together under the open window, and the mad moth beat against the chimney of the lamp. What sounds long silent, what scents fallen odorless, renew themselves in the contents of these records! They are parts of the universal death, which, unless we call it the universal life, we are for-ever dying into. They who equally with myself composed the Atlantic, the beloved, the admired contributors, outdied me, so many of them, years and years ago. The great Agassiz, who wept to think he should not finish his book, stayed to give the magazine only a few first chapters. It was but the other year that the wise, the good Shaler, whose writing in it began almost with mine, ceased from it; and now Aldrich, my time-mate, my work-mate, my play-mate, is gone, he who should have died hereafter, how long hereafter! For the greater great, they who were still living presences when the enterprise which their genius had stamped with ineffaceable beauty and dignity was safe in its strong maturity, the tears were dried years ago. If one outlives, one loses, one sorrows and ceases to sorrow. That is the law. I cannot wish that these intimates in the ideal and the real had outlived the least of their friends, but I wish they had not died till the work which they, far more than any editor, or all the editors, created, was crowned with the end of its half-hundredth year.

I did not well know how to begin these wandering lucubrations—I believe I never used the word before, but it is not too late—and I do not know better how to end them. But the reader may care to learn how it was with one when he parted with the task which had so intensely occupied him for fifteen years. When the burden dropped from me, it was instantly as if I had never felt it. I did not think of it enough to miss it, to rejoice that it was gone. After another fifteen years I began to dream of resuming it. I would dream that I was on the train from New York to Boston, going back to be editor of the Atlantic again. The dream went on, fitfully or frequently, for five or six years. Then at last I found myself on the train with one of my successors, not the least of my friends, and I said, "Well, Scudder, I have often dreamed of going back to be editor of the Atlantic, and here, now, I am really going." But that was a dream, too.

John William De Forest (1826—1906)

When in 1867 the assistant editor of the *Atlantic Monthly* wrote a review of *Miss Ravenel's Conversion,* he himself had published no novel. John William De Forest, some eleven years Howells' senior, was already known for his study of Connecticut Indians, for several travel books on Europe and the Orient, and for two or three novels; moreover, he had recently published in *Harper's Monthly* some vivid descriptions of the battles of the Civil War based on his own experience. At the outbreak of the war, when Howells sailed for Italy as United States consul in Venice, De Forest returned from Europe to recruit a company of volunteers in New Haven, with whom he served for the next four years. The letters De Forest wrote home to his family during these campaigns in Louisiana and the Shenandoah were the basis for his first important novel, *Miss Ravenel's Conversion from Secession to Loyalty*.

Among the books that came to his hand after his return from Italy, Howells tells us, was *Miss Ravenel's Conversion,* which he recognized at once as "the best novel suggested by the civil war"—indeed, one of the best American novels he had known. Though Howells at once conceived a "passion" for the book and for all the books that De Forest was to write, he was never able to make the public care for them as much as he did, a fact he considered more discreditable to the taste of the times than to the talent of the author. It is to Howells' credit, certainly, that in *My Literary Passions* he hailed De Forest as "one of our foremost novelists, for his keen and accurate touch in character, his wide scope, and his unerring rendition of whatever he has attempted to report of American life." *Kate Beaumont* (1872), *The Wetherel Affair* (1873), *Honest John Vane* (1875), and others, Howells reviewed without ever persuading "either critics or readers to think with me." In *Harper's Bazar,* October, 1901, Howells attributed De Forest's lack of popular success to a "sort of disdainful honesty" and a "certain scornful bluntness" which, he said, was not appreciated by women, who formed the larger portion of the novel readers of the nineteenth century.

So strong was the public feeling against the realism of De Forest's description of war that Harper's, having purchased *Miss Ravenel's Conversion* for $1,250, for serial publication in 1865, decided not to risk it in the magazine; instead, Harper's published the novel in 1867 in book form. As Gordon Haight points out in his 1939 edition of the story, De Forest was writing a "realism not generally acceptable in America until after World War I." Howells, however, recognized at once that the "inexorable veracity" of this firsthand report of the Civil War made De Forest "really the only American novelist" so far to appear.

Howells' review of *Miss Ravenel's Conversion*, printed below, makes the reader perceive that in admiring De Forest's realism, Howells was learning how he himself might make use of this new, more direct approach to real people in actual situations. The shock of meeting recognizable people in novels—"his soldiers are the soldiers we actually know"—far outweighed in Howells' mind any interest in plot, which he passed over with a glance. Haight suggests, indeed, that Howells was sufficiently impressed with the character of Colonel Carter to convert him, minus a uniform, into the Bartley Hubbard of *A Modern Instance* (1882), and remarks that "Howells borrowed De Forest's theme of a fine young girl, who, against her father's advice, married a man of weak character and lived to regret it; but he refined it to the taste of genteel readers." Whether one agrees with Haight as to the refinement of Bartley Hubbard, one can certainly see in Colonel Carter, "with his brown eyes at once audacious and mirthful," more than a suggestion of Hubbard. It is not impossible that an early reading of De Forest deepened Howells' concept of what realism in character might imply.

The writer who affected most profoundly Howells' sense of the importance of truth in novel writing was Tolstoy, whom, Howells tells us, he read for the first time in 1886. A letter from De Forest to Howells, published in *Harper's*, May, 1887, shows us that Howells' enthusiasm for Tolstoy was caught by De Forest. Howells quoted from the letter of De Forest, naming him "a writer who is one of our chief novelists, and who was one of our bravest soldiers": "You do right to praise Tolstoy," wrote De Forest in this significant letter. "Something that you wrote a while ago sent me to his *Peace and War* [sic]. . . . Let me tell you that nobody but he has written the whole truth about war and battle." In "The Editor's Study" of the following September, Howells compared De Forest with Tolstoy, "the incomparable," "as presenting an image of American life" in *Miss Ravenel's Conversion* that might be placed beside Tolstoy's *War and Peace*, without shrinking it to "pitiful dimensions." "It is an admirable novel," Howells remarked, "and spacious enough for the vast drama glimpsed in it."

Howells again spoke of De Forest's "Tolstoyan fidelity" in his review of De Forest's *Lover's Revolt* in *Literature* for December, 1898. It is, Howells writes, "in infinitely smaller compass, a story akin to 'War and Peace' through the moral quality of truth to universal and eternal human experience." His comments on De Forest in "The New Historical Romances," in the *North American Review*, December, 1900, show that Howells, as a mature and experienced critic, found in De Forest "the artistic conscience of a true novelist"; this he had sensed when, as a young reviewer on the *Atlantic*, he first read *Miss Ravenel's Conversion*. De Forest's novels remained for him a "passion," for he read them not only to fill his column, but also to catch from the author the new "strong" realistic approach to novel writing. In *Heroines of Fiction*, written the year after his essay in the *North American Review*, Howells expressed the hope that "in some future moment" De Forest's "belated turn" would come. Howells himself had long recognized De Forest as "a novelist whose work has in some respects not only not been surpassed, but not approached, among us—a realist before realism was named."

THE STAMP OF VERITY*

The light, strong way in which our author goes forward in this story from the first, and does not leave difficulty to his readers, is pleasing to those accustomed to find an American novel a good deal like the now extinct American stage-coach, whose passengers not only walked over bad pieces of road, but carried fence-rails on their shoulders to pry the vehicle out of the sloughs and miry places. It was partly the fault of the imperfect roads, no doubt, and it may be that our social ways have only just now settled into such a state as makes smooth going for the novelist; nevertheless, the old stage-coach was hard to travel in, and what with drafts upon one's good nature for assistance, it must be confessed that our novelists have been rather trying to their readers. It is well enough with us all while the road is good,—a study of individual character, a bit of landscape, a stretch of well-worn plot, gentle slopes of incident; but somewhere on the way the passengers are pretty sure to be asked to step out,—the ladies to walk on ahead, and the gentlemen to fetch fence-rails.

Our author imagines a Southern loyalist and his daughter sojourning in New Boston, Barataria, during the first months of the war. Dr. Ravenel has escaped from New Orleans just before the Rebellion began, and has brought away with him the most sarcastic and humorous contempt and abhorrence of his late fellow-citizens, while his daughter, an ardent and charming little blonde Rebel, remembers Louisiana with longing and blind admiration. The Doctor, born in South Carolina, and living all his days among slaveholders and slavery, has not learned to love either; but Lillie differs from him so widely as to scream with joy when she hears of Bull Run. Naturally she cannot fall in love with Mr. Colburne, the young New Boston lawyer, who goes into the war conscientiously for his country's sake, and resolved for his own to make himself worthy and lovable in Lillie's blue eyes by destroying and desolating all that she holds dear. It requires her marriage with Colonel Carter—a Virginia gentleman, a good-natured drunkard and *roué* and soldier of fortune on our side—to make her see Colburne's worth, as it requires some comparative study of New Orleans and New Boston, on her return to her own city, to make her love the North. Bereft of her husband by his own

* *Miss Ravenel's Conversion from Secession to Loyalty,* by J. W. De Forrest, 1867. Review in the *Atlantic Monthly,* July, 1867. (In the edition reviewed the author's name was spelled De Forrest.)

wicked weakness, and then widowed, she can at last wisely love and marry Colburne; and, cured of Secession by experiencing on her father's account the treatment received by Unionists in New Orleans, her conversion to loyalty is a question of time duly settled before the story ends.

We sketch the plot without compunction, for these people of Mr. De Forrest's are so unlike characters in novels as to be like people in life, and none will wish the less to see them because he knows the outline of their history. Not only is the plot good and very well managed, but there is scarcely a feebly painted character or scene in the book. As to the style, it is so praiseworthy that we will not specifically censure occasional defects,—for the most part, slight turgidities notable chiefly from their contrast to the prevailing simplicity of the narrative.

Our war has not only left us the burden of a tremendous national debt, but has laid upon our literature a charge under which it has hitherto staggered very lamely. Every author who deals in fiction feels it to be his duty to contribute towards the payment of the accumulated interest in the events of the war, by relating his work to them; and the heroes of young-lady writers in the magazines have been everywhere fighting the late campaigns over again, as young ladies would have fought them. We do not say that this is not well, but we suspect that Mr. De Forrest is the first to treat the war really and artistically. His campaigns do not try the reader's constitution, his battles are not bores. His soldiers are the soldiers we actually know,—the green wood of the volunteers, the warped stuff of men torn from civilization and cast suddenly into the barbarism of camps, the hard, dry, tough, true fibre of the veterans that came out of the struggle. There could hardly be a better type of the conscientious and patriotic soldier than Captain Colburne; and if Colonel Carter must not stand as type of the officers of the old army, he must be acknowledged as true to the semi-civilization of the South. On the whole he is more entertaining than Colburne, as immoral people are apt to be to those who suffer nothing from them. "His contrasts of slanginess and gentility, his mingled audacity and *insouciance* of character, and all the picturesque ins and outs of his moral architecture, so different from the severe plainness of the spiritual temples common in New Boston," do take the eye of peace-bred Northerners, though never their sympathy. Throughout, we admire, as the author intends, Carter's thorough and enthusiastic soldiership, and we perceive the ruins of a generous nature in his aristocratic Virginian pride, his Virginian profusion, his imperfect Virginian sense of honor. When he comes to be shot, fighting bravely at the head of his column, after having swindled his government, and half unwillingly done his worst to break his wife's heart, we feel that our side has lost a good soldier, but that the world is on the whole something better for our loss. The reader must go to the novel itself for a perfect conception of this character, and preferably to those dialogues in which Colonel Carter so freely takes part; for in his development of Carter, at least, Mr. De Forrest is mainly dramatic. Indeed, all the talk in the book is free and natural, and, even without the hard swearing which distinguishes the speech of some, it would be difficult to mistake one speaker for another, as often happens in novels.

The character of Dr. Ravenel, though so simple, is treated in a manner invariably delightful and engaging. His native purity, amiability, and generosity, which a life-long contact with slavery could not taint; his cordial scorn of Southern ideas; his fine and flawless instinct of honor; his warmhearted courtesy and gentleness, and his gayety and wit; his love of his daughter and of mineralogy; his courage, modesty, and humanity,—these are the traits which recur in the differing situations with constant pleasure to the reader.

Miss Lillie Ravenel is as charming as her adored papa, and is never less nor more than a bright, lovable, good, constant, inconsequent woman. It is to her that the book owes its few scenes of tenderness and sentiment; but she is by no means the most prominent character in the novel, as the infelicitous title would imply, and she serves chiefly to bring into stronger relief the traits of Colonel Carter and Doctor Ravenel. The author seems not even to make so much study of her as of Mrs. Larue, a lady whose peculiar character is skilfully drawn, and who will be quite probable and explicable to any who have studied the traits of the noble Latin race, and a little puzzling to those acquainted only with people of Northern civilization. Yet in Mrs. Larue the author comes near making his failure. There is a little too much of her,—it is as if the wily enchantress had cast her glamour upon the author himself,—and there is too much anxiety that the nature of her intrigue with Carter shall not be misunderstood. Nevertheless, she bears that stamp of verity which marks all Mr. De Forest's creatures, and which commends to our forbearance rather more of the highly colored and strongly-flavored parlance of the camps than could otherwise have demanded reproduction in literature. The bold strokes with which such an amusing and heroic reprobate as Van Zandt and such a pitiful poltroon as Gazaway are painted, are no less admirable than the nice touches which portray the Governor of Barataria, and some phases of the aristocratic, conscientious, truthful, angular, professorial society of New Boston, with its young college beaux and old college belles, and its life pure, colorless, and cold to the eye as celery, yet full of rich and wholesome juices. It is the goodness of New Boston, and of New England, which, however unbeautiful, has elevated and saved our whole national character; and in his book there is sufficient evidence of our author's appreciation of this fact, as well as of sympathy only and always with what is brave and true in life.

Mark Twain (1835—1910)

Among "the good things" that "began to come out of the West" in the 1860's and 1870's were the manuscripts of a certain Mark Twain, known to Howells as Clemens. As assistant editor of the *Atlantic Monthly*, Howells had eagerly welcomed and reviewed *Innocents Abroad* before its redheaded author strolled into the Boston office late in the winter of 1869 to thank the editor in person. This meeting marked the beginning of a friendship that lasted until Clemens' death in 1910.

Innocents Abroad was based on the reports Clemens had sent back to the *Alta-California* and the New York *Herald* and *Tribune* of a trip he had taken in 1867 with a party of excursionists to the Mediterranean and the Holy Land. The only other book he had published was *The Celebrated Frog of Calaveras County and Other Sketches* (1867). Howells, who took boundless delight in both books, did not hesitate to announce in the last sentence of his review of *Innocents Abroad:* "It is no business of ours to fix his rank among the humorists California has given us, but we think he is, in an entirely different way from all the others, quite worthy of the company of the best."

Clemens and Howells have both left us descriptions of their notable meeting. More to our purpose here is the account of the interview by Clemens' biographer, Albert Bigelow Paine, for in this paragraph is suggested something of the literary relationship immediately established by the two men.

[Mark Twain's] manner, his humor, his quaint colloquial forms all delighted Howells—more, in fact, than the opulent sealskin overcoat which he affected at this period . . . startling enough, we may believe, in the conservative atmosphere of the *Atlantic* rooms. And Howells—gentle, genial, sincere—filled with the early happiness of his calling, won the heart of Mark Twain and never lost it, and, what is still more notable, won his absolute and unvarying confidence in all literary affairs. It was always Mark Twain's habit to rely on somebody, and in matters pertaining to literature and to literary people in general he laid his burden on William Dean Howells from that day.

In a letter to T. B. Aldrich in 1871, Clemens tells us that it was Bret Harte on whom he relied before he met Howells: "Bret Harte trimmed and trained and schooled me patiently until he changed me from an awkward utterer of coarse grotesqueness to a writer of paragraphs and chapters that have found a certain favor in the eyes of even some of the very decentest people in the land." We know, moreover, that Olivia Langdon, whom Clemens married in 1870, helped him edit the proof sheets of *Innocents Abroad* before Howells saw the book, and she continued to "edit" her husband until her death in 1905. What part Howells played in the curbing of his friend's "bold fancy" and "breadth of parlance" no one, not even Howells himself, could say. In *My Mark Twain*, Howells attempted to define their difference of character, and hence of style:

Throughout my long acquaintance with him his graphic touch was always allowing itself a freedom which I cannot bring my fainter pencil to illustrate. He had the Southwestern, the Lincolnian, the Elizabethan breadth of parlance, which I suppose one ought not to call coarse without calling one's self prudish; and I was often hiding away in discreet holes and corners the letters in which he had loosed his bold fancy.

That Howells' "fainter pencil" was an effective editorial weapon against Clemens' extravagances, is quite evident from Howells' remark in *My Mark Twain* on Clemens' association with him as a contributor to the *Atlantic*:

When Clemens began to write for it he came willingly under its rules, for with all of his wilfulness there never was a more biddable man in things you could show him reason for. . . . If you wanted a thing changed, very good, he changed it; if you suggested that a word or a sentence or a paragraph had better be struck out, very good, he struck it out.

Clemens relied on Howells completely, and in 1875 he took the manuscript of *Tom Sawyer* to him to read, "as a friend and critic, and not as an editor." For Clemens counted on Howells' unfailing appreciation of his humor, his realism, his naturalness of style, his common sense. Clemens soon learned the importance of a favorable review from the editor of the *Atlantic*. *Roughing It* (1872), *Sketches Old and New* (1875), *The Adventures of Tom Sawyer* (1876), *A Tramp Abroad* (1880), and all the others, were reviewed by Howells, one by one, as they came off the press. So powerful was Howells' criticism, even while he was still on the *Atlantic*, that, as Clemens tells us in his *Autobiography:*

> More than once I took the precaution of sending my book, in manuscript, to Mr. Howells, when he was editor of the *Atlantic Monthly* so that he could prepare a review of it at leisure. I knew that he would say the truth about the book—I also knew that he would find more merit than demerit in it, because I already knew that that was the condition of the book. I allowed no copy of that book to go out to the press until after Mr. Howells's notice of it had appeared. That book was always safe. There wasn't a man behind a pen in all America that had the courage to find anything in the book which Mr. Howells had not found—there wasn't a man behind a pen in America that had spirit enough to say a brave and original thing about the book on his own responsibility.

Amusingly practical as the above paragraph shows Clemens to have been, we know that his literary relationship with Howells was far more complex. He depended on Howells not merely for favorable book reviews, but even more for his deep understanding of the inner intent of his humorous-tragic, realistic-romantic, exuberant-commonsense, and altogether individual way of writing.

Because Howells shows in his essay in the *North American*

Review of February, 1901, his appreciation of the whole range of contradictory characteristics that mark Clemens' manner and style, we have selected a portion of this essay rather than one of his earlier *Atlantic* reviews. The occasion for the article "Mark Twain: An Inquiry" was the publication of a "uniform edition" of his writings, and also, Howells adds, "his return to his own country after an absence so long as to form a psychological perspective in which his characteristics make a new appeal." Clemens had, in fact, recently brought to a close the famous round-the-world lecture tour that had enabled him to recover from bankruptcy. The "psychological perspective" through which Howells tells us he viewed the characteristics of Clemens in 1901 gives us a portrait perhaps more finely shaded than critics in our generation remember.

Howells himself included this essay in *My Mark Twain*, with the brief introductory remark that the reviews in the book, arranged chronologically, begin "rather stiffly, pedantically, and patronizingly, but that they grow suppler, wiser, and more diffident as they go on." We realize, as we read this essay, that the perspective Howells had gained extended beyond Clemens to the "characteristics" of the colloquial, native, honest realism, closely related to romance, for which Howells fought for so many years. Clemens summed up the movement, but with a difference that was genius, and this Howells recognized.

MARK TWAIN: AN INQUIRY*

[Mark Twain's] great charm is his absolute freedom in a region where most of us are fettered and shackled by immemorial convention. He saunters out into the trim world of letters, and lounges across its neatly kept paths, and walks about on the grass at will, in spite of all the signs that have been put up from the beginning of literature, warning people of dangers and penalties for the slightest trespass.

* *North American Review,* February, 1901.

One of the characteristics I observe in him is his single-minded use of words, which he employs as Grant did to express the plain, straight meaning their common acceptance has given them with no regard to their structural significance or their philological implications. He writes English as if it were a primitive and not a derivative language, without Gothic or Latin or Greek behind it, or German and French beside it. The result is the English in which the most vital works of English literature are cast, rather than the English of Milton, and Thackeray, and Mr. Henry James. I do not say that the English of the authors last named is less than vital, but only that it is not the most vital. It is scholarly and conscious; it knows who its grandfather was; it has the refinement and subtlety of an old patriciate. You will not have with it the widest suggestion, the largest human feeling, or perhaps the loftiest reach of imagination, but you will have the keen joy that exquisite artistry in words can alone impart, and that you will not have in Mark Twain. What you will have in him is a style which is as personal, as biographical as the style of any one who has written, and expresses a civilization whose courage of the chances, the preferences, the duties, is not the measure of its essential modesty. It has a thing to say, and it says it in the word that may be the first or second, or third choice, but will not be the instrument of the most fastidious ear, the most delicate and exacting sense, though it will be the word that surely and strongly conveys intention from the author's mind to the reader's. It is the Abraham Lincolnian word, not the Charles Sumnerian; it is American, Western.

Now that Mark Twain has become a fame so world-wide, we should be in some danger of forgetting, but for his help, how entirely American he is, and we have already forgotten, perhaps, how truly Western he is, though his work, from first to last, is always reminding us of the fact. But here I should like to distinguish. It is not alone in its generous humor, with more honest laughter in it than humor ever had in the world till now, that his work is so Western. Any one who has really known the West (and really to know it one must have lived it), is aware of the profoundly serious, the almost tragical strain which is the fundamental tone in the movement of such music as it has. Up to a certain point, in the presence of the mys-

tery which we call life, it trusts and hopes and laughs; beyond
that it doubts and fears, but it does not cry. It is more likely
to laugh again, and in the work of Mark Twain there is little
of the pathos which is supposed to be the ally of humor, little
suffusion of apt tears from the smiling eyes. It is too sincere
for that sort of play; and if after the doubting and the fearing
it laughs again, it is with a suggestion of that resentment
which youth feels when the disillusion from its trust and hope
comes, and which is the grim second-mind of the West in the
presence of the mystery. It is not so much the race-effect as
the region-effect; it is not the Anglo-American finding expression, it is the Westerner, who is not more thoroughly the
creature of circumstances, of conditions, but far more dra-
matically their creature, than any prior man. He found himself placed in them and under them, so near to a world in
which the natural and primitive was obsolete, that while he
could not escape them, neither could he help challenging
them. The inventions, the appliances, the improvements of
the modern world invaded the hoary eld of his rivers and for-
ests and prairies, and while he was still a pioneer, a hunter, a
trapper, he found himself confronted with the financier, the
scholar, the gentleman. They seemed to him, with the world
they represented, at first very droll, and he laughed. Then
they set him thinking, and as he never was afraid of anything,
he thought over the whole field, and demanded explanations
of all his prepossessions, of equality, of humanity, of representative government and revealed religion. When they had
not their answers ready, without accepting the conventions of
the modern world as solutions or in any manner final, he
laughed again, not mockingly, but patiently, compassionately.
Such, or somewhat like this, was the genesis and evolution of
Mark Twain.

Missouri was Western, but it was also Southern, not only in
the institution of slavery, to the custom and acceptance of
which Mark Twain was born and bred without any applied
doubt of its divinity, but in the peculiar social civilization of
the older South from which his native State was settled. It
would be reaching too far out to claim that American humor,
of the now prevailing Western type, is of Southern origin, but
without staying to attempt it I will say that I think the fact

could be established; and I think one of the most notably Southern traits of Mark Twain's humor is its power of seeing the fun of Southern seriousness, but this vision did not come to him till after his liberation from neighborhood in the vaster far West. He was the first, if not the only man of his section, to betray a consciousness of the grotesque absurdities in the Southern inversion of the civilized ideals in behalf of slavery, which must have them upside down in order to walk over them safely. No American of Northern birth or breeding could have imagined the spiritual struggle of Huck Finn in deciding to help the negro Jim to his freedom, even though he should be forever despised as a negro thief in his native town, and perhaps eternally lost through the blackness of his sin. No Northerner could have come so close to the heart of a Kentucky feud, and revealed it so perfectly, with the whimsicality playing through its carnage, or could have so brought us into the presence of the sardonic comi-tragedy of the squalid little river town where the store-keeping magnate shoots down his drunken tormentor in the arms of the drunkard's daughter, and then cows with bitter mockery the mob that comes to lynch him. The strict religiosity compatible in the Southwest with savage precepts of conduct is something that could make itself known in its amusing contrast only to the native Southwesterner, and the revolt against it is as constant in Mark Twain as the enmity to New England orthodoxy is in Dr. Holmes. But he does not take it with such serious resentment as Dr. Holmes is apt to take his inherited Puritanism, and it may be therefore that he is able to do it more perfect justice, and impart it more absolutely. At any rate there are no more vital passages in his fiction than those which embody character as it is affected for good as well as evil by the severity of the local Sunday-schooling and church-going. . . .

Slavery in a small Missouri river town could not have been the dignified and patriarchal institution which Southerners of the older South are fond of remembering or imagining. In the second generation from Virginia ancestry of this sort, Mark Twain was born to the common necessity of looking out for himself, and while making himself practically of another order of things he felt whatever was fine in the old and could regard whatever was ugly and absurd more tolerantly, more humorously than those who bequeathed him their enmity to it. Fortunately for him, and for us who were to enjoy his humor, he came to his intellectual consciousness in a world so large and free and safe that he could be fair to any wrong while seeing the right so unfailingly; and nothing is finer in him than his gentleness with the error which is simply passive and negative. He gets fun out of it, of course, but he deals almost tenderly with it, and hoards his violence for the superstitions and traditions which are arrogant and active. His pictures of that old river-town, Southwestern life, with its faded and tattered aristocratic ideals and its squalid democratic realities, are pathetic, while they are so unsparingly true and so inapologetically and unaffectedly faithful.

The West, when it began to put itself into literature, could do so without the sense, or the apparent sense, of any older or politer world outside of it; whereas the East was always looking fearfully over its shoulder at Europe, and anxious to account for itself as well as represent itself. No such anxiety as this entered Mark Twain's mind, and it is not claiming too much for the Western influence upon American literature to say that the final liberation of the East from this anxiety is due to the West, and to its ignorant courage or its indifference to its difference from the rest of the world. It would not claim to be superior, as the South did, but it could claim to be humanly equal, or rather it would make no claim at all, but would simply be, and what it was, show itself without holding itself responsible for not being something else.

The Western boy of forty or fifty years ago grew up so close to the primeval woods or fields that their inarticulate poetry became part of his being, and he was apt to deal simply and uncritically with literature when he turned to it, as he dealt with nature. He took what he wanted, and left what he did not like; he used it for the playground, not the workshop of his spirit. Something like this I find true of Mark Twain in peculiar and uncommon measure. I do not see any proof in his books that he wished at any time to produce literature, or that he wished to reproduce life. When filled up with an experience that deeply interested him, or when provoked by some injustice or absurdity that intensely moved him, he burst forth, and the outbreak might be altogether humorous, but it was more likely to be humorous with a groundswell of seriousness carrying it profoundly forward. In all there is something curiously, not very definably, elemental, which again seems to me Western. He behaves himself as if he were the first man who was ever up against the proposition in hand.

Edward Eggleston (1837—1902)

In the *Atlantic Monthly* of March, 1872, Howells reviewed a best seller by an obscure Methodist circuit rider from Indiana who had begun his literary career as a writer of Sunday-school stories. *The Hoosier Schoolmaster,* by Edward Eggleston, had appeared the previous December in book form after having been serialized in fourteen issues of *Hearth and Home.* The little volume achieved an immediate and unexpected success; 10,000 copies were sold in this country in the first six months after publication. Howells hailed the book as "a picture of manners hitherto strange to literature," reflecting "the rudeness and ugliness of the intermediate West." The story, he said, is well told in "a plain fashion," though the reader does foresee the "fortunate ending." Other reviews of *The Hoosier Schoolmaster* appeared in the same month, both in *Harper's* and in *Scribner's,* but the editor of the *Atlantic* was the only critic to point out the false pathos of some of Eggleston's characterizations, as well as to commend him for his village types and local dialect.

Before the appearance of *The Hoosier Schoolmaster,* Howells had written to Eggleston congratulating him on his story, "Huldah, the Help," and pronouncing it "a very unaffected bit of good work." As though in reply, Eggleston had cited Howells in the July 6, 1871, issue of the *Independent* as among those men "who will do justice to the customs and speech of the West." When Eggleston made a hurried visit to Boston the following December, he called on Howells and wrote home to his wife, "Saw Mr. Howells to-day and am to dine in his beautiful cottage to-morrow." No doubt the recently appointed editor of the *Atlantic* and the supervising editor of the *Independent* had much to talk about, for they had many things in common besides the fact that they were ambitious young journalists from the "intermediate West" who had escaped from the limitations of their small towns by means of writing.

Both Howells and Eggleston were then venturing into the

writing of sketches based on their own experiences. At the time when Eggleston's account of his younger brother's experiences in teaching were appearing in *Hearth and Home,* Howells was making literary copy for the *Atlantic* of his own daily observations (published in 1871 as *Suburban Sketches*). But there the similarity between the two writers ended, for Howells, after all, was the author of *Italian Journeys,* a lecturer at Harvard, and editor of the *Atlantic.* Eggleston, a Methodist preacher by training and a writer by chance, had scarcely read a novel before he happened to write a best seller in an attempt to rescue an expiring magazine.

Howells greeted Eggleston's next novel, *The End of the World,* in his review for the *Atlantic* of December, 1872, with the same blend of praise and blame he had accorded *The Hoosier Schoolmaster.* This "natural story teller," Howells remarked, made use of materials that were "simple and even common," but by his sincerity in observing the scene around him, presented the reader with new characters and threw "the shadow of a grand dramatic element" across the ordinary plot. A cursory glance at the *Independent,* for which Eggleston was writing at this period, indicates that he was conscious of a wide range of social and political issues of the day but that his literary interests did not go beyond the roster of well-known American names, Irving, Poe, Hawthorne, Emerson, Lowell, and Holmes.

Howells' own appreciation of the value of "everyday experience and common homespun," on the other hand, came not only from his early Ohio experience, but also from the reading at this time of the novels of Björnson and Turgenev. As we have seen in Part I, Howells, between 1869 and 1870, reviewed Björnson as the herald of "the new way of writing" and in 1872 praised Turgenev's *Smoke* in similar terms. What Howells admired in the technique of the Europeans was that they reflected the life about them, that they wasted no words in explaining their characters, and that they never sentimentalized. When Howells reviewed Eggleston's third novel, *The Circuit Rider,* in the *Atlantic* of June, 1874, he took him to task, with Björnson as his authority, for pausing to comment on his characters. "This is bad art, as Mr. Eggleston himself must feel," Howells wrote, bringing home the lesson of Björnson to this "natural story teller" with an instinct for Indiana dialect and frontier incident, but with no knowledge of the European writers engaged in similar quests. The review of *The Circuit Rider,* printed below, shows better than any other how Howells grafted critical ideas from abroad on native stock.

Though Eggleston was unaware of the European realist from whom Howells was gathering hints both as critic and writer, he had read Hippolyte Taine, whose *Philosophy of Art in the Netherlands* he reviewed briefly in the *Independent* of December 8, 1870. His younger brother tells us that Eggleston "set forth his theory of art—that the artist, whether with pen or brush, who would do his best work, must choose his subjects from the life he knows. He cited the Dutch painters." Interestingly enough, Howells reviewed the same Taine book in the *Atlantic* of March, 1871, but, imbued as he was with the writings of Björnson and Turgenev, he found Taine's work, though entertaining, "of no great original value." He remarked, "The considerations of race are not new nor striking; perhaps they are rather conventional." In February, 1872, Howells reviewed Taine's *History of English Literature,* which he found disappointing, especially Taine's concept of the study of art, about which Howells himself had ideas. In the August issue of the *Atlantic* for the same year Howells commented on Taine's *Notes on the English,* pointing out that Emerson and Hawthorne had done the same thing better. Since Howells as a novelist found Taine's descriptions of English types amusing, he laid aside the book with "penitential distrust"; Taine's "distorted philosophy" seemed to Howells only "lucky thrusts in the dark."

Though the reading of Taine's *Philosophy of Art in the Netherlands* might have contributed to Eggleston's resolve to write of his own countryside, it was Björnson and Turgenev whose literary techniques enabled Howells both to criticize and to praise the novelist from Indiana. In *Harper's* of February, 1889, he reviewed one of Eggleston's later novels, *The Graysons,* which he considered one of his best works, for "the story deals with elements that lie about us like earth and water." In this review, written in the thick of the battle for realism, Howells was reminded again of his "literary passion" of former days, especially for Björnson, who not only influenced Howells' own style, but, through Howells, helped to establish a basis for commenting on the "new way of writing," of which *The Hoosier Schoolmaster* is a humble example.

FLAT CREEK*

In Mr. Eggleston's "Hoosier Schoolmaster" we are made acquainted with the rudeness and ugliness of the intermediate West, after the days of pioneering, and before the days of civilization,—the West of horse-thief gangs and of mobs, of protracted meetings and of extended sprees, of ignorance drawn slowly through religious fervors towards the desire of knowledge and decency in this world. The scene of the story is in Hoopole County, Indiana, a locality which we hope the traveller would now have some difficulty in finding, and in a neighborhood settled, apparently, by poor whites from Virginia and Kentucky, sordid Pennsylvania Dutchmen, and a sprinkling of 'cute dishonest Yankees. The plot is very simple and of easy prevision from the first, being the struggles of Ralph Hartsook with the young idea in the district school on Flat Creek, where the twig was early bent to thrash the schoolmaster. He boards round among the farmers, starting with "old Jack Means," the school trustee, whose son Bud, the most formidable bully among his pupils, he wins over to his own side, and whose daughter, with her mother's connivance, falls in love with him and resolves to marry him. But the schoolmaster loves their bound girl Hannah, and makes enemies of the mother and daughter; and they are not slow to aid in the persecution which rises against him, and ends in his arrest for a burglary committed by the gang of the neighborhood, including some of the principal citizens of Flat Creek. Of course it comes out all right, though the reader is none the less eager because he foresees the fortunate end. The

---

* *The Hoosier Schoolmaster*, by Edward Eggleston, 1871. Reviewed in the *Atlantic Monthly*, March, 1872.

story is very well told in a plain fashion, without finely studied
points. It is chiefly noticeable, however, as a picture of manners hitherto strange to literature, and the characters are interesting as part of the picture of manners, rather than as
persons whose fate greatly concerns us; yet they all have a
movement of their own, too, and are easily known from each
other,—which is much for characters. One of the best is old
Mrs. Means, who is also one of the worst in another sense.
Her talk is the talk of all Flat Creek; and we cannot suggest
the dialect in which the conversation of the story is chiefly
written better than by giving a speech of hers:—"Here Mrs.
Means stopped to rake a live coal out of the fire with her
skinny finger, and then to carry it in her skinny palm to the
bowl—or to the *hole*—of her cobpipe. When she got the smoke
agoing she proceeded:

" 'You see this ere bottom land was all Congress land in
them there days, and it sold for a dollar and a quarter, and I
says to my ole man, "Jack," says I, "Jack, do you git a plenty
while you're a gittin'. Git a plenty while you're a gittin',"
says I, "fer 'twon't never be no cheaper'n 'tis now," and it
ha'nt been, I knowed 'twouldn't,' and Mrs. Means took the
pipe from her mouth to indulge in a good chuckle at the
thought of her financial shrewdness. " 'Git a plenty while
you're a gittin',' says I. I could see, you know, they was a
powerful sight of money in Congress land. That's what made
me say, "Git a plenty while you're a gittin'." And Jack, he's
wuth lots and gobs of money, all made out of Congress land.
Jack didn't git rich by hard work. Bless you, no! Not him.
That a'n't his way. Hard work a'n't, you know. 'Twas that air
six hundred dollars he got along of me, all salted down into
Flat Crick bottoms at a dollar and a quarter a acre, and 'twas
my sayin', "Git a plenty while you're a gittin'," as done it.'
And here the old ogre laughed, or grinned horribly, at Ralph,
showing her few straggling, discolored teeth.

"Then she got up and knocked the ashes out of her pipe,
and laid the pipe away and walked round in front of Ralph.
After adjusting the 'chunks' so that the fire would burn, she
turned her yellow face toward Ralph, and scanning him closely came out with the climax of her speech in the remark,

'You see as how, Mr. Hartsook, the man what gits my Mirandy'll do well. Flat Crick land's worth nigh upon a hundred a acre.' "

We should say the weak side of Mr. Eggleston's story was the pathos that gets into it through some of Little Shocky's talk, and the piety that gets into it through Bud Means; and we mean merely that these are not so well managed as the unregeneracy, and not at all that they are not good things to have in a story. The facts about Shocky are touching enough, and the facts about Bud most respectable.

Mr. Eggleston is the first to touch in fiction the kind of life he has represented, and we imagine that future observers will hardly touch it in more points. Its traits seem to be all here, both the good and the bad; but that it is a past or passing state of things is sufficiently testified by the fact, to which Mr. Eggleston alludes in his Preface, that the story, as it appeared serially, was nowhere more popular than in Southern Indiana. Flat Creek, Hoopole County, would not, we imagine, have been so well pleased thirty years ago with a portrait which, at any rate, is not flattered.

A TALE OF THE HEROIC AGE*

No American story-teller has of late years had greater success, of a good kind, than Mr. Eggleston, who in four years has given us consecutively, The Hoosier Schoolmaster, The End of the World, The Mystery of Metropolisville, and now The Circuit Rider. His books have been read by the hundred thousands; they have been respectfully considered by the most difficult criticism amongst us, they have been translated, we believe, and misunderstood in the Revue des Deux Monds,[13] they have enjoyed the immortality of English republication. They merited as much. They were exceedingly well theorized. Mr. Eggleston considered the vast fields of fiction lying untouched in the region of his birth and the home

* The Circuit Rider: A Tale of the Heroic Age, by Edward Eggleston, 1874. Reviewed in the Atlantic Monthly, June, 1874.

of his early manhood, and for his plots, scenes, and characters, he acted on Mr. Greeley's famous advice, and went West.
It must have been that he truthfully painted the conditions
and people whom he aimed to portray, for it was in the West
that his popularity began, and it is there doubtless that it is
now the greatest. He does not deal with the contemporary
West, but with the West of forty or fifty years ago; and except in The Mystery of Metropolisville he does not leave the
familiar ground of the Ohio Valley. The scene of his first two
stories is in Southern Indiana, that of the last is in Southern
Ohio. On this ground he was at home, yet he was able to
view all the people and situations from the outside, and in the
light of subsequent life in the East. Some disadvantages came
from this advantage. He was too conscious of the oddity of
his material, and he placed an inartistic stress upon unimpor-
tant details of dialect, customs, and character. Even in The
Circuit Rider, he stops from time to time, in the description of
some rude or grotesque scene, to make the reader an ironical
or defiant apology for treating of such unrefined matters; or,
if he has some wild incident or trait to handle, pauses to ex-
patiate upon it and caress its singularity. This is bad art, as
Mr. Eggleston must himself feel, and he ought not to indulge
it. The novelist's business is to paint such facts of character
and custom as he finds so strongly that their relative value in
his picture will be at once apparent to the reader without a
word of comment: otherwise his historical picture falls to the
level of the panorama with a showman lecturing upon the
striking points and picking them out for observance with a
long stick. It is not in this way that the masters of the art
which Mr. Eggleston reveres accomplish their results. Björnson does not add a word to impress on our imaginations the
Norwegian incidents and characters he sets before us in *Arne;*
and Turgénieff, in such a Russian tale as The Lear of the
Steppes, leaves all comment to the reader. Everything necessary to the reader's intelligence should be quietly and artfully
supplied, and nothing else should be added.

We speak the more frankly of this blemish in Mr. Eggleston's last work because we find The Circuit Rider such a vast
advance upon his former stories. The Mystery of Metropolisville was disappointing; for though it showed a good sense of

character and the story was interesting, it was not so fresh as The Hoosier Schoolmaster, and it had not such poetic elements as The End of the World. It was not an advance; it was something of a retrogression. But in our pleasure with The Circuit Rider we have been willing to forget this, and we are glad to recognize the author in his most fortunate effort. The story is of backwoods life in Ohio at the time when the Methodists began to establish the foundations of their church in the new land, among the children of the Indian-fighters and pioneers, and the hero of the story is one of those ardent young preachers who throughout the Southwest were known as circuit riders. They were each given a certain field of labor by the Conference, and they traveled on horseback from point to point in this field, preaching, praying, and turning sinners to repentance, and at due seasons assembling their forces in mighty camp-meetings, and gathering whole neighborhoods into the capacious bosom of their church at once. No history is more picturesque or dramatic than theirs, and Mr. Eggleston has well called their time the heroic age.

Henry James (1843—1916)

"Talking of talks: young Henry James and I had a famous one last evening, two or three hours long, in which we settled the true principles of literary art," Howells wrote to Edmund Clarence Stedman on December 5, 1866. Though James was at that time only twenty-three years old, Howells, the recently appointed assistant editor of the *Atlantic Monthly*, recognized at once the quality of the young man, six years his junior, about whom he was writing to his New York friend. "He is a very earnest fellow," the letter continued, "and I think extremely gifted—gifted enough to do better than any one has yet done toward making us a real American novel." Surely a remarkable prediction concerning James, who, in December, 1866, had to his credit only a scattering of reviews and stories published in three or four magazines.

The famous talks between Howells and James took place in the course of "nocturnal rambles," which began in the summer of 1866 and "followed one another into the mild autumnal weather." The Jameses had arrived in Cambridge six months after the Howellses had settled into "Cottage Quiet," 41 Sacramento Street. Though the aimless strolls of the two young writers were frequent enough, they met more often in Howells' small house, for James liked to talk over his stories with Howells and his wife and to read aloud from his manuscript by the light of a kerosene lamp. Even more important to the young James, Howells was eager to accept from him all the stories he could supply, in spite of the misgivings of his "senior editor, Mr. Fields."

Beginning with James's review of Howells' *Italian Journeys*, for the January, 1868, issue of the *North American Review*, and ending with Howells' discussion of James's *Hawthorne* in the *Atlantic Monthly* for February, 1880, James and Howells continued to exchange critical views in a series of seven articles in the *Atlantic*, the *North American Review*, the *Independent*, and the *Nation* before Howells resigned from the *Atlantic* and before James took up his permanent

163

residence in London. Through these reviews, three by Howells and four by James, one can trace some of the "principles of literary art" that the two writers explored together in the days when both were experimenting in the novel form. The difference between romanticism and romance; the symbolism of Hawthorne; the realism of Balzac; the psychological insight of George Eliot; the technique of Turgenev; the richness of the European scene as contrasted with the provincialism of Concord and Boston; "the great American novel" and who should write it—all these questions and many more were raised by Howells and James in the reviews of each other's books as they were published. Were not the same questions discussed in the strolls around Fresh Pond in the summer of 1866 and by the side of the air-tight stove in Howells' parlor in the following winter? Before Howells himself went to Europe in 1882, he wrote "Henry James, Jr." for *Century Magazine*, which one may read as a conclusion to the talks begun more than fifteen years earlier.

The most important of these seven essays, Howells' review of Henry James's small book on Hawthorne, is given below. Since it was Howells who, in the course of their Cambridge rambles, had directed James's attention to Hawthorne, he must have studied with particular interest James's presentation of this New England author to the British public in Morley's "English Men of Letters" series in 1879.

Howells' review of James's essay is in a sense a continuation of the earlier conversations that must frequently have touched on the general question of the provincial tone of the American scene and the position of the writer in such a society. Howells' essay begins with a discussion of James's remarks on the exquisite provinciality of Hawthorne. Is it provincial for an Englishman to be English, a Frenchman to be French, or an American to be American? Howells' question no doubt reflects not only his argument with James as to the narrowness of Hawthorne's experience, but also the prolonged discussions between Howells and James themselves as to whether the American soil was sufficiently rich to nourish an American novelist. By the time James wrote his essay on Hawthorne he had definitely decided to abandon his American roots and to establish himself in England; Howells had come to the op-

posite decision and some of his reasons are reflected in the review. Though Howells and James continued to correspond for
the remainder of their lives, though they exchanged their
latest books and visited one another in London, Cambridge,
and New York, the significant period of their relationship
came to a close at the time when each one made his basic
decision as to his relation to his native land.

Not only does Howells take issue with James on the subject of Hawthorne's provinciality but he also points out to him
"the confusion which, for some reason not made clear, he
permits himself" in his discussion of Hawthorne's definition
of romance, to be found in the preface to *The House of the
Seven Gables*. The romance and the novel, Howells pointed
out with some impatience, are as distinct as the poem and
the novel. Since Howells, as James's critic and editor, had
urged him to correct the exaggerated analytical realism of
his early stories by a touch of romance as defined by Hawthorne, and since James in several stories he had submitted to
the *Atlantic* followed Howells' advice, one can understand the
asperity of Howells in his remarks on James's apparent confusion.

James's unwillingness to accept the sharp distinction between romance and realism, the romance and the novel, is at-
tributable to the fact that at the time when Howells was urging upon James a reconsideration of the romances of Hawthorne, James was introducing to Howells the realistic novels
of Balzac. These studies of the Comédie Humaine Howells
discussed in his review of James's *French Poets and Novelists*
in the *Atlantic* of July, 1878, a discussion which he continued in Sections III and V of *Criticism and Fiction*. Immense
as Balzac undoubtedly was as a realist, Balzac unfortunately
was not always Balzac, and when he erred it was in terms of
romantic exaggeration. Reading his romance *Le Père Goriot*—
"it is not worthy the name of novel"—is to discover that Balzac's realism, like that of Dickens, is profoundly romantic,
"full of malarial restlessness, wholly alien to healthful art."
On the other hand, Hawthorne's romance is merely the poetic
atmosphere cast over his essentially realistic probing of the
human heart and is truer to experience than Balzac's "realistic" overstatement. So, at least, ran Howells' part in the dia-

logue, a portion of which is found in the essay below.

Thus the dialogue continued between these two novelists bent on discovering the "true principles of literary art." Howells' review of James's *Hawthorne* is but one speech in this conversation, which began in 1866 and ended for a time in 1882, when both authors were prepared to write their greatest novels. Here we are concerned with the first and more inseminating chapter of this friendship, which in fact lasted until James's death in 1916, or, more truly, until Howells' death in 1920, for he left unfinished an essay to be called "The American James."

JAMES'S HAWTHORNE*

Mr. James's book on Hawthorne, in Morley's English Men of Letters series, merits far closer examination and carefuller notice than we can give it here, alike for the interest of its subject, the peculiarity of its point of view, and the charm and distinction of its literature. An American author writing of an American author for an English public incurs risks with his fellow-countrymen which Mr. James must have faced, and is much more likely to possess the foreigner whom he addresses with a clear idea of our conditions than to please the civilization whose portrait is taken. Forty-six, fifty, sixty-four, are not dates so remote, nor are Salem and Concord societies so extinct, that the people of those periods and places can be safely described as provincial, not once, but a dozen times; and we foresee, without any very powerful prophetic lens, that Mr. James will be in some quarters attainted of high treason. For ourselves, we will be content with saying that the provinciality strikes us as somewhat over-insisted upon, and that, speaking from the point of not being at all provincial ourselves, we think the epithet is sometimes mistaken. If it is not provincial for an Englishman to be English, or a Frenchman French, then it is not so for an American to be

* *Hawthorne*, by Henry James, 1879. Reviewed in the *Atlantic Monthly*, February, 1880.

American; and if Hawthorne was "exquisitely provincial," one
had better take one's chance of universality with him than
with almost any Londoner or Parisian of his time. Provinciality, we understand it, is a thing of the mind or the soul;
but if it is a thing of the experiences, then that is another matter, and there is no quarrel. Hawthorne undoubtedly saw less
of the world in New England than one sees in Europe, but
he was no cockney, as Europeans are apt to be.

At the same time we must not be thought to deny the value
and delightfulness of those chapters on Salem and Brook
Farm and Concord. They are not very close in description,
and the places seem deliciously divined rather than studied.
But where they are used unjustly, there will doubtless be abundant defense; and if Salem or Brook Farm be mute, the welkin
will probably respond to the cries of certain critics who lie in
wait to make life sorrowful to any one dealing lightly with the
memory of Thoreau or the presence of the poet Channing.
What will happen to a writer who says of the former that he
was "worse than provincial, he was parochial," and of the latter that he resembles the former in "having produced literary
compositions more esteemed by the few than by the many,"
we wait with the patience and security of a spectator at an
auto da fé, to see. But even an unimbattled outsider may suggest that the essential large-mindedness of Concord, as expressed in literature, is not sufficiently recognized, although it
is thoroughly felt. The treatment of the culture foible and of
the colorless aesthetic joys, the attribution of "a great deal of
Concord five and thirty years ago" to the remark of a visitor
of Hawthorne that Margaret Fuller "had risen perceptibly into a higher state of being since their last meeting," are exquisite,—too exquisite, we fear, for the sense of most Englishmen,
and not too fine only for the rarefied local consciousness
which they may sting. Emerson is indeed devoutly and amply
honored, and there is something particularly sweet and tender
in the characterization of such surviving Brook Farmers as
the author remembers to have met; but even in speaking of
Emerson, Mr. James has the real misfortune to call his grand
poem for the dedication of the monument to Concord Fight a
"little hymn." It is little as Milton's sonnet on Shakespeare is
little.

We think, too, that in his conscience against brag and *chauvinism* Mr. James puts too slight a value upon some of Hawthorne's work. It is not enough to say of a book so wholly unexampled and unrivaled as The Scarlet Letter that it was "the finest piece of imaginative writing put forth in" America; as if it had its parallel in any literature. When he comes to speak of the romances in detail, he repairs this defect of estimation in some degree; but here again his strictures seem somewhat mistaken. No one better than Mr. James knows the radical difference between a romance and a novel, but he speaks now of Hawthorne's novels, and now of his romances, throughout, as if the terms were convertible; whereas the romance and the novel are as distinct as the poem and the novel. Mr. James excepts to the people in The Scarlet Letter, because they are rather types than persons, rather conditions of the mind than characters; as if it were not almost precisely the business of the romance to deal with types and mental conditions. Hawthorne's fictions being always and essentially, in conception and performance, romances, and not novels, something of all Mr. James's special criticism is invalidated by the confusion which, for some reason not made clear, he permits himself. Nevertheless, his analysis of the several books and of the shorter tales is most interesting; and though we should ourselves place The Blithedale Romance before The House of Seven Gables, and should rank it much higher than Mr. James seems to do, we find ourselves consenting oftener than dissenting as we read his judgments. An admirably clear and just piece of criticism, we think, is that in which he pronounces upon the slighter and cheaper *motif* of Septimius Felton. But here there are not grounds for final sentence; it is possible, if that book had received the author's last touches, it might have been, after all, a playful and gentle piece of irony rather than a tragedy.

What gives us entire satisfaction, however, is Mr. James's characterization, or illustrations of Hawthorne's own nature. He finds him an innocent, affectionate heart, extremely domestic, a life of definite, high purposes singularly unbaffled, and an "unperplexed intellect." The black problem of evil, with which his Puritan ancestors wrestled concretely, in groans and despair, and which darkens with its portentous shadow nearly everything that Hawthorne wrote, has become his literary material; or, in Mr. James's finer and more luminous phrase, he "transmutes this heavy moral burden into the very substance of the imagination." This strikes us as beautifully reasonable and true, and we will not cloud it with comment of ours. But satisfactorily as Mr. James declares Hawthorne's personality in large, we do not find him sufficient as to minor details and facts. His defect, or his error, appears oftenest in his discussion of the note-books, where he makes plain to himself the simple, domestic, democratic qualities in Hawthorne, and yet maintains that he sets down slight and little aspects of nature because his world is small and vacant. Hawthorne noted these because he loved them, and as a great painter, however full and vast his world is, continues to jot down whatever strikes him as picturesque and characteristic. The disposition to allege this inadequate reason comes partly from that confusion of the novelist's and the romancer's work of which we have spoken, and partly from a theory, boldly propounded, that it needs a long history and "a complex social machinery to set a writer in motion." Hawthorne himself shared, or seemed to share, this illusion, and wrote The Marble Faun, so inferior, with its foreign scene, to the New England romances, to prove the absurdity of it. As a romancer, the twelve years of boyhood which he spent in the wild solitudes of Maine were probably of greater advantage to him than if they had been passed at Eton and Oxford. At least, until some other civilization has produced a romantic genius at all comparable to his, we must believe this. After leaving out all those novelistic "properties," as sovereigns, courts, aristocracy, gentry, castles, cottages, cathedrals, abbeys, universities, museums, political class, Epsoms, and Ascots, by the absence of which Mr. James suggests our poverty to the English conception, we have the whole of human life remaining, and a social structure presenting the only fresh and novel opportunities left to fiction, opportunities manifold and inexhaustible. No man would have known less what to do with that dreary and worn-out paraphernalia than Hawthorne.

We can only speak of the excellent comment upon Hawthorne's Old Home, and the skillful and manly way in which Mr. James treats of that delicate subject to his English audi-

ence. Skillful and manly the whole book is,—a miracle of
tact and of self-respect, which the author need not fear to
trust to the best of either of his publics. There is nothing to regret in the attitude of the book; and its literature is always a
high pleasure, scarcely marred by some evidences of hurry,
and such *writerish* passages as that in which *sin* is spoken of
as "this baleful substantive with its attendant adjective."

It is a delightful and excellent essay, refined and delicate in
perception, generous in feeling, and a worthy study of the
unique romancer whom its closing words present with justice
so subtle and expression so rich:—

"He was a beautiful, natural, original genius, and his life
had been singularly exempt from worldly preoccupations and
vulgar efforts. It had been as pure, as simple, as unsophisti-
cated, as his work. He had lived primarily in his domestic
affections, which were of the tenderest kind; and then—without eagerness, without pretension, but with a great deal of
quiet devotion—in his charming art. His work will remain; it
is too original and exquisite to pass away; among the men of
imagination he will always have his niche. No one has had just
that vision of life, and no one has had a literary form that
more successfully expressed his vision. He was not a moralist,
and he was not simply a poet. The moralists are weightier,
denser, richer, in a sense; the poets are more purely incon-
clusive and irresponsible. He combined in a singular degree
the spontaneity of the imagination with a haunting care for
moral problems. Man's conscience was his theme, but he saw
it in the light of a creative fancy which added, out of its own
substance, an interest, and, I may almost say, an importance."

John Hay (1838—1905)

The Bread-Winners: A Social Study appeared serially in *Century Magazine*—where it "did not lack comment more or less impassioned"—from August, 1883 to January, 1884, when it was issued by Harper's in book form. John Hay, biographer of Lincoln, ambassador to Great Britain, and twice Secretary of State, did not during his life admit that he was also the author of this much-discussed novel. Nor did Howells ever acknowledge that he wrote the review of *The Bread-Winners*, signed "W," for the May, 1884, issue of *Century*. However, the authorship of this early review can hardly be doubted after a consideration of "John Hay in Literature," written for the *North American Review*, September, 1905, soon after the death of Hay. In this essay Howells looked back over his long friendship with Hay, which had begun twenty-five years before the publication of *The Bread-Winners*, and referred to their meeting in London while Hay was writing the book. Almost unconsciously, Howells threw light on the anonymity of his earlier review in his later essay.

John Hay wrote his "social study" in about four months' time in the summer of 1882 and asked Howells to read it while he and his family were in London, enjoying association with Henry James, Bret Harte, Thomas Bailey Aldrich, James Osgood, and others. Howells hoped to persuade Aldrich to accept the manuscript for the *Atlantic*, since he himself had recently written *The Stillwater Tragedy*, another anti-labor novel. Aldrich refused it, however, because Hay insisted on anonymity, perhaps following the lead of his friend Henry Adams, who, four years earlier, had not acknowledged his authorship of *Democracy*. After the serializing of *The Bread-Winners* in the *Century*, Hay explained, in an unsigned letter to that magazine, why it seemed important to him not to declare his name: "a working man" himself, he was also a businessman, he pointed out, and could not afford to endanger his relationship with either group. Howells, in the 1905 essay cited above, continued to guard Hay's secret, referring only to "a piece of fiction" that he had found Hay writing in London in 1882, and which Hay asked him to read. Though many guessed the authorship of Hay's novel, it was not officially disclosed until 1907.

When Hay and Howells met in London during the summer of 1882, both men had reached an important milestone in their careers, as they probably realized. Howells had resigned his editorship of the *Atlantic* and had recently published his most important novel up to that time, *A Modern Instance;* Hay, having started his career as poet, essayist, and journalist, had become a successful businessman and, in 1877, Assistant Secretary of State under President Hayes. To understand why Hay turned from writing to business, then to politics, and why in 1882 he wrote *The Bread-Winners* from a violently antilabor angle, one must know something of the personal life of the author.

In 1875 Hay moved to Cleveland as a young newspaper man and married the daughter of the railroad millionaire, Amasa Stone. Hay soon gave up journalism, entered his father-in-law's business, and proved himself a very capable man of affairs at a time when Amasa Stone stood in need of help. Stone, who began life as a simple carpenter interested in building bridges for westward-moving pioneers, was estimated to have lost over a million and a half dollars in the depression of 1873, which followed the great industrialization and capital expansion of the post-Civil War period. The plight of labor, caught between inflated prices and depreciated currency, brought on the wave of strikes, especially at railroad centers such as St. Louis, Pittsburgh, and Cleveland, that made many think the "Revolution" had arrived in this country. John Hay, as an associate of Stone, was deeply concerned with these railroad strikes; in two long anonymous letters to the *Century* in answer to the critics of *The Bread-Winners,* Hay explained how he had gathered all the material for the novel from the daily newspapers of Cleveland, St. Louis, and elsewhere at the time of the strikes of 1877. "I contend," he wrote, "that the book is true, and was written with an honest purpose"— which was to warn the public against the "foreign" labor agitators, who, he said, exploited the industrious and contented workers of Anglo-Saxon origin. Hay insisted that he was not opposed to trade unions, which seemed to many a threat to the country, but to the self-interested labor leaders, the new villain of American fiction proposed by the anonymous writer. Moreover, Hay felt, it was the duty of the novelist to utter public warnings when he clearly perceived danger.

Howells, in his review of *The Bread-Winners* for the *Century,* applauded this interpretation of the novelist's responsibility. If the author of *The Bread-Winners* means only to tell the truth about his characters, if he refuses to flatter either the employer or the workingman, "he has done the cause of labor and the cause of art both a service." Critical realism meant, at this time as well as later, that morality, truth, and art are all one and the same. Howells' only objection to Hay's novel, from the point of view of realism, had to do with the happy ending, which seemed to him untrue and therefore artistically false.

When "W" admitted that "we should have been well content to see the strike of the telegraphers succeed," he spoke as a citizen rather than as a critic, and expressed views that diverged from those of the author of *The Bread-Winners.* The strike to which Howells referred took place in July, 1883, just one month before the serializing of Hay's novel in the *Century.* Since Amasa Stone was at that time on the board of directors of Western Union, a position that John Hay filled after the death of his father-in-law the following May, we may be sure that Hay was not among those who would have been content to see the strikers win. The strikers did, in fact, lose, and Hay continued to sit on the board until he resigned to become ambassador to Great Britain.

Again in his essay, "John Hay in Literature," Howells touched on his essential disagreement with Hay on labor questions, as well as on the realistic treatment of character in novels. In this essay he looked back to the publication of *The Bread-Winners,* and observed: "It dealt with the labor question in the old persuasion concerning united labor, and it cannot be found a modern criticism of economic conditions." Howells' social thinking was so at variance with that of Hay that the very platform of the Society of Bread-Winners—"The downfall of the money power, the rehabilitation of labor, the

organization for mutual profit"—which is satirized by Hay, is
accepted by Howells as the basis of life in Altruria. What
Howells appreciated in *The Bread-Winners* was the range of
new characters set before the reader of fiction, rather than
the antiunion attitude of the author—"the sketches of the local
politicians, the leaders who can swing their wards." Hay's
genius turned us from "our provisional gentility" toward our
"crude potentialities," just as Howells' was to do in the social
novels that came soon after *The Bread-Winners*. For the notable books Howells reviewed not only helped him define his
critical beliefs but also inspired him to further fictional experiments of his own, such as *A Hazard of New Fortunes*. On
Hay's strikers Howells commented: "It is quite time we were
invited to consider some of them in fiction as we saw some of
them in fact during the great railroad strike"; and as a novelist he followed the suggestion.

A SOCIAL STUDY*

This story did not lack comment, more or less impassioned,
during the course of its publication in THE CENTURY, and
its characteristics will probably have been canvassed still more
thoroughly before these pages meet the eye of the reader.
From the first it was noticeable that the criticism it received
concerned the morality of the story, and even the morality of
the writer, rather than the art of either; and, on the whole,
we do not see why this was not well enough. It was, we think,
a wholesome way of regarding the performance, and, even in
those who most disliked it, implied a sense of conscience and
of thinking in the book, however warped, however mistaken.
It was a better way of looking at it than a mere survey of its
literary qualities would have been, and it marked an advance
in popular criticism. The newspapers did not inquire so much
whether this or that character was well drawn, this or that incident or situation vividly reported, as whether the writer,

* *The Bread-Winners: A Social Study*, 1884. Review in the
Century Magazine, May, 1884.

dealing forcibly with some living interests of our civilization, meant one thing or another by what he was doing; though they did not fail to touch upon its literature at the same time. The discussion evolved an interesting fact, which we recommend to all intending novelists, that among us at least the novelist is hereafter to be held to account as a public teacher, that he must expect to be taken seriously, and must do his work with the fear of a community before his eyes which will be jealous of his ethical soundness, if nothing else. What did the author of "The Bread-winners" mean by making his rich and well-to-do people happy, and leaving all the suffering to the poor? Does he believe that it is wrong for the starving laborer and operative to strike? Are his sympathies with the rich against the poor? Does he think workingmen are all vicious? Does he mean that it was right for Captain Farnham to kiss Maud Matchin when she had offered herself to him in marriage and dropped herself into his arms, unless he meant to marry her? Was he at all better than she if he could do such a thing? Was it nice of Mrs. Belding to tell her daughter of this incident? Ought Alice Belding to have accepted him after such a thing as that?

Some of these voices—which still agitate the air—are unmistakably soprano and contralto; some, for which we have less respect, are falsetto. We do not know whether it would be possible, or whether it would be profitable, to answer them conclusively. At any rate, we shall not attempt it; but we would like to call attention to the very important fact that the author of "The Bread-winners" shows no strong antipathy to strikers till they begin to burn and rob and propose to kill; and we will ask the abstract sympathizer to recall his own sensations in regard to the great railroad strike in 1877, after the riots began. In our own mind there is no question that any laborer, or any multiple of him, not being content with his hire, has the right to leave his work; and we should have been well content to see the strike of the telegraphers succeed, and not ill pleased to see those who thought them paid enough put to live awhile on their wages. But if the striking telegraphers, like the striking railroad men, had begun to threaten life and destroy property, we should have wanted the troops called out against them. We cannot see that the author of "The Bread-

winners" has gone beyond this point in his treatment of the
question of strikes.

We cannot see, either, that he has in any sort a prejudice
against the workingman as a workingman. We are all workingmen in America, or the sons of workingmen, and few of us
are willing to hear them traduced; but, for our own part,
they do not seem to us preeminent for wisdom or goodness,
and we cannot perceive that they derive any virtue whatever
from being workingmen. If they were lawyers, doctors, or
clergymen, they would be equally respectable, and not more
so. They are certainly better than the idle rich, as they are better than the idle poor—the two classes which we have chiefly,
if not solely, to dread; and it is the idle poor whom our author
does not like, whom he finds mischievous, as other writers of
romance have long found the idle rich. It is the Offitts and the
Botts and the Bowersoxes whom he detests, not the Matchins,
nor even the Sleenys. These are treated with respect, and
Sleeny, at least in the end, is rather more lavishly rewarded
than any of the millionaires, if his luck in escaping the gal-
lows is not more than neutralized by the gift of Miss Maud
Matchin as a wife. But there is no doubt the author meant
well by him; and we think there is no doubt that he means
well by all honest, hard-working people. He has not made
them very brilliant, for still "the hand of little employment
hath the nicer sense"; he has not heaped them with worldly
prosperity, and it must be owned that Divine Providence has
done no better by them. Let us be just before we are generous, even to the workingman. Let us recognize his admirable
qualities in full measure; but let us not make a fetich of him,
impeccable, immaculate, infallible. We suspect that in portraying a certain group of people as he has done, the author
of "The Bread-winners" meant no more nor less than to tell
the truth about them; and if he has not flattered the likeness
of his workingmen, he has done the cause of labor and the
cause of art both a service. Workingmen are in no bad way
among us. They have to practice self-denial and to work hard,
but both of these things used to be thought good for human
nature. When they will not work, they are as bad as club men
and ladies of fashion, and perhaps more dangerous. It is quite
time we were invited to consider some of them in fiction as

we saw some of them in fact during the great railroad strike.

When we come to the question whether Captain Farnham ought to have kissed Maud Matchin, or turned from her with loathing, we confess that we feel the delicacy of the point. Being civilians, we will venture to say that we fear it was quite in character for an ex-army man to kiss her, and so far the author was right. Whether it was in character for a perfect gentleman to do so, we cannot decide; something must be conceded to human nature and a sense of the girl's impudence, even in a perfect gentleman. But, having dodged this point, we feel all the more courage to deal with another, namely, whether he was not quite as bad as she. We think not, for reasons which his accusers seem to forget. Miss Matchin did not offer herself to him because she loved him, but because she loved his wealth and splendor, and wished to enjoy them, and though she was careful to tell him that she would only be his wife, it is not clear to our minds that if she could have been equally secure of his wealth and splendor in another way, there was anything in her character to make her refuse. He did behave with forbearance and real kindness to that foolish and sordid spirit; he did use her with magnanimity and do what he could to help her, though she had forfeited all claim upon his respect. He may not have been a perfect gentleman, but he was certainly a very good sort of man, in spite of that questionable kiss.

We might wish to have Miss Matchin other than she was for her own sake; but if she were different, she would not be so useful nor so interesting. She is the great invention, the great discovery, of the book; and she is another vivid and successful study of American girlhood, such as it seems to be largely the ambition of our novelists to make. She is thoroughly alive, caught by an instantaneous process, in which she almost visibly breathes and pulsates. One has a sense of her personal presence throughout, though it is in the introductory passages that we realize most distinctly her mental and spiritual qualities, and the wonderful degree in which she is characterized by American conditions—by the novels of the public library, by the ambitious and inadequate training of the high school, by the unbounded freedom of our social life. These conditions did not produce her; with other girls they are the agencies of inestimable good. But, given the nature of Miss Maud Matchin, we see the effect upon her at every point. We can see the effect, also, of the daily newspaper and of the display of Algonquin Avenue, with its histories in brick and stone of swift, and recent, and immeasurable riches. The girl's poetry is money, her romantic dream is to marry a millionaire. She has as solid and sheer a contempt for the girl who dreams of an old-fashioned hero and love in a cottage as she has for her hard-working father and mother. There are no influences in her home to counteract the influences from without. She grows up a beautiful, egotistic, rapacious, unscrupulous fool. But take the novels and the high school away, and she would still have been some kind of fool. The art of the author consists in having painted her as she exists through them. The novelist can do no more. He shows us this creature, who is both type and character, and fitly leaves the moralist to say what shall be done about her. Probably nothing can be done about her at once; but if she is definitely ascertained as a fact of our civilization, it is a desirable step in self-knowledge for us.

At the end the author's strong hand seems to falter a little in the treatment of Miss Matchin. We read of her "rosy and happy face" when the man she has driven to murder is acquitted, and the chief weakness of the book here betrays itself. Something should have been done to show that those people had entered hand in hand into their hell, and that thenceforth there could be no hope for them.

There are some admirable passages of casual or subordinate interest in the book, and a great many figures drawn with a force that leaves a permanent impression. The episode of Maud's canvass for the place in the public library, and her triumph through the "freeze-out" that leaves Pennybaker "kickin' like a Texas steer"; the behavior of the rascal mayor during the strike; all the politicians' parlance; the struggle of Alice Belding with herself after her good-natured but not very wise mother has told her of Maud's offer to Farnham; her feeling that this has somehow stained or "spoiled" him;—these are traits vigorously or delicately treated, that may be set against an account of less interesting handling of some society pictures. The scenes of the riot and the attack on Farnham's house are stirringly done; that of the murderous attack on Farnham by Offitt less so; and it appears to us rather precipitate in Alice to fall asleep as soon as she hears that her lover is not fatally hurt. But these are very minor points. Generally speaking, we think the author has done what he meant to do. We believe that he has been faithful to his observation of facts. If the result is not flattering, or even pleasing, that is not his fault, and neither his art nor his morality is to blame for it.

Edward Bellamy (1850—1898)

"I do not think it by any means a despicable thing to have hit the popular fancy of our enormous commonplace average," Howells wrote in an essay for the *North American Review* of December, 1900, commenting on the popularity of "The New Historical Romances." In this essay he looked back sadly at "the welter of overwhelming romance" that had inundated the book market during the very period when "the natural tendency" in fiction prevailed. It was not, Howells insisted, that these historical romances "hit the popular fancy" that made them "despicable." "Some of the best and truest books have done this"—*Pilgrim's Progress,* for instance, *Uncle Tom's Cabin,* and *Roughing It;*—"Edward Bellamy's gospel of justice in *Looking Backward* did it." What was really lamentable was "to have hit the popular fancy and not to have done anything to change it, but everything to fix it." Romance that "flatters with false dreams of splendor" is false romance.

Bellamy's posthumous romance, *The Duke of Stockbridge* (written in part by Bellamy in 1879 and finished by his cousin, the Rev. Francis Bellamy, in 1900) is an example of the kind of romance Howells admired. For this historical romance is concerned with "the short and simple annals of the poor" in "that squalid period immediately following the Revolution" and reflects the real feelings of the common man. For the same reason Howells considered *Dr. Heidenhoff's Process* (1880) one of "the finest feats in the region of romance" that he had ever read; here the author's imagination worked on "the level of average life, and built the fabric of its dreams out of common clay."

Howells wrote the memorial essay reprinted below for the *Atlantic Monthly* soon after the early death of Bellamy in 1898, and it was reprinted in October of the same year as a preface to the posthumous collection of Bellamy's short stories, *The Blindman's World and Other Stories.* The essay not only tells us of the life and work of this modest, retiring man from Chicopee Falls, Massachusetts, but also reflects

Howells' idea that romance is justified only if the feelings of "the average man" are woven into "the webs of fancy." The action of Bellamy's romances, Howells pointed out, always took place in the atmosphere of the American village. Bellamy spent most of his life in the village of Chicopee Falls, except for a year in Germany as a youth and a brief period in Boston, where he studied for the law before becoming, in 1880, a journalist in New York City and in Springfield, Massachusetts. Always more interested in his romances than in journalism, he soon returned to live and write in his native village.

Bellamy's full-length romance, *Miss Ludington's Sister* (1884), Howells reviewed in *Century Magazine* for August, 1884, commenting on the air of reality that marked it. Possibly this review served to introduce Howells to Bellamy, for shortly after its appearance Bellamy wrote to Howells elaborating his idea of the relationship between romance and realism. "Whether I belong to the school of realists or not I do not know," he wrote.

> It is the business of the author to write as the spirit moves, and of the critic to classify him. But my own belief is that while the warp, that is the framework and main lines of the story, should be the author's own invention, the woof and filling should be supplied from his observations of the real life about him. It is the undertaking of the romancer to give an air of reality even to the unreal.

Perhaps Howells had this letter of 1884 in mind when he observed in his essay that Bellamy "does not so much transmute our every day reality to the substance of romance as make the airy stuff of dreams one in quality with veritable experience." This is the secret of Bellamy's "singular art," and also of the art of Hawthorne, the other "great romancer" admired by Howells.

Howells presided at the Bellamy memorial meeting held in the Social Reform Club of New York, June 7, 1898. On that occasion he remarked: "We know him best as a social agitator, and we do not value him enough as a literary man."

The following essay is important primarily as a just appraisal of the imaginative literary power of Bellamy; it should also be read as a comment on Bellamy's social ideas by the man who wrote *A Traveler from Altruria* (1894). Since the novelist, Mr. Twelvemough, in Howells' utopian romance, is undoubtedly a satiric partial portrait of the author himself, and since the traveler, Mr. Homos, cites Bellamy as the source of his information, we can assume that their conversation is a reflection of the lively exchange of ideas that took place between Bellamy and Howells from 1884 to 1894.

"I know him not only in his books, but also in his life, and it is there that I grew to love him," Howells told the Social Reform Club. Whether he was also familiar with a curious little essay, *The Religion of Solidarity*, written by Bellamy in 1874 but not published until 1940, one does not know; certainly the thought of the essay was familiar to him. "We are a part of all" and are saved from "self-hood" only by recognizing that fact, wrote Bellamy, expressing the basic philosophy of Howells' "complicity," first suggested in 1887 in *The Minister's Charge* and fully explored in *A Traveler from Altruria*. Bellamy and Howells were both aware of the waves of Comtian positivism that stressed the religion of brotherhood in the new age of science (the very word "altruism" was first used by Comte), but Bellamy seems to have supplied the practical thought that Howells needed for his less clearly formulated social feeling.

In 1886, when Howells' life was changed, he tells us, by his reading of Tolstoy, Bellamy was in search of a program for the reform of society. Bellamy wrote:

According to my best recollections, it was in the fall or winter of 1886 that I sat down to my desk with the definite purpose of trying to reason out a method of economic organization by which the republic might guarantee the livelihood and material welfare of its citizens on the basis of equality corresponding to and supplanting their political equality.

The public stand that Howells took in 1887 against the execution of the Chicago Anarchists, when he risked his position as editor and novelist by a letter of protest to the New York *Tribune,* indicates that his social concern was then sufficiently strong to make him anxious to learn all he could of practical schemes for the reform of society. Howells eagerly read and reviewed *Looking Backward (Harper's,* June, 1888), noting its kinship with Gronlund's *Cooperative Commonwealth,* which he had reviewed two years earlier. He "was at that time deeply moved by the social injustice which we had all recently discovered," Garland reports in "Meetings with Howells." He added, "Often as we walked and talked he spoke of Bellamy's delineation of the growing contrast between rich and poor." Howells, Bellamy, Gronlund, Garland, and others were meeting during the winters of 1889—1891 to discuss these new ideas at the Church of the Carpenter, in Boston, of which W. D. P. Bliss, the well-known Christian Socialist, was minister.

Bellamy's picture of the social inequalities of modern American society influenced Howells' scenes in *A Hazard of New Fortunes,* on which he was working when Bellamy's *Looking Backward* was making the best-seller list and Bellamy Clubs (later called Nationalist Clubs) were being formed all over the country. "I cannot refrain from congratulating you upon *The Hazard of New Fortunes,"* Bellamy wrote Howells when the serial began to appear in *Harper's Weekly* in March, 1889. "I have read the last number with enthusiasm. You are writing what everyone is thinking and all the rest will have to follow or lose their readers."

The enthusiasm with which Bellamy read Howells' novel was deepened by the fact that Howells and Bellamy frequently met in Boston during the winters of 1889, 1890, and 1891. Howells was present at the organization meeting of the first Nationalist Club of Boston, December 1, 1888. Both men were interested in the Society of Christian Socialists, inaugurated in 1889 in the same city under the leadership of the liberal Episcopal priest, the Rev. W. D. P. Bliss, and Howells also attended the opening by Bliss of the Church of the Carpenter, April 13, 1890. Not only Bellamy and Howells but also Edward Everett Hale, Laurence Gronlund, Hamlin Garland, and other reformers met and discussed the new economic and social ideas in the light of Christianity.

Though the Nationalist Club retained its essentially economic outlook and the Society of Christian Socialists its religious orientation, the membership of both groups overlapped and their ideas, as reflected in their publications, *The Nationalist* and *The Dawn,* were closely related. *A Traveler From Altruria* contains many of Bellamy's economic ideas, but the Christian thought suffusing it may be traced to Howells' association with the Society of Christian Socialists in Boston.

Bellamy was so enthusiastic about Howells' utopia that he wrote a special article about it in *The New Nation,* November 26, 1892, and reviewed it again in the October 14, 1893, issue, when *A Traveler* was completed. In a congratulatory letter to Howells, Bellamy signed himself, "Yours in the sympathy of a common aspiration." Both men had been drawn into the discussions of Boston liberal thinkers, who "revived throughout Christendom the faith in a millennium," as Howells said in the following essay, and both men hoped through their utopian romances to affect the thinking of "our enormous commonplace average."

THE ROMANTIC IMAGINATION*

The first book of Edward Bellamy's which I read was Dr. Heidenhoff's Process, and I thought it one of the finest feats in the region of romance which I had known. It seemed to me all the greater because the author's imagination wrought in it on the level of average life, and built the fabric of its dream out of common clay. The simple people and their circumstance were treated as if they were persons whose pathetic story he had witnessed himself, and he was merely telling it. He wove into the texture of their sufferings and their sorrows the magic thread of invention so aptly and skillfully that the reader felt nothing improbable in it. One even felt a sort of moral necessity for it, as if such a clue not only could be, but must be given for their escape. It became not merely probable, but imperative, that there should be some means of ex-

* Essay in the *Atlantic Monthly,* August, 1898.

tirpating the memory which fixed a sin in lasting remorse, and of thus saving the soul from the depravity of despair. When it finally appeared that there was no such means, one reader, at least, was inconsolable. Nothing from romance remains to me more poignant than the pang that this plain, sad tale imparted.

The art employed to accomplish its effect was the art which Bellamy had in degree so singular that one might call it supremely his. He does not so much transmute our every-day reality to the substance of romance as make the airy stuff of dreams one in quality with veritable experience. Every one remembers from Looking Backward the allegory which figures the pitiless prosperity of the present conditions as a coach drawn by slaves under the lash of those on its top, who have themselves no firm hold upon their places, and sometimes fall, and then, to save themselves from being ground under the wheels, spring to join the slaves at the traces. But it is not this, vivid and terrible as it is, which most wrings the heart; it is that moment of anguish at the close, when Julian West trembles with the nightmare fear that he has been only dreaming of the just and equal future, before he truly wakes and finds that it is real. That is quite as it would happen in life, and the power to make the reader feel this like something he has known himself is the distinctive virtue of that imagination which revived throughout Christendom the faith in a millennium.[14]

A good deal has been said against the material character of the happiness which West's story promises men when they shall begin to do justice, and to share equally in the fruits of the toil which operates life; and I confess that this did not attract me. I should have preferred, if I had been chooser, to have the millennium much simpler, much more independent of modern inventions, modern conveniences, modern facilities. It seemed to me that in any ideal condition (the only condition finally worth having) we should get on without most of these things, which are but sorry patches on the rags of our outworn civilization, or only toys to amuse our greed and vacancy. Aesthetically, I sympathized with those select spirits who were shocked that nothing better than the futile luxury of their own selfish lives could be imagined for the lives which overwork and underpay had forbidden all pleasures; I acquired considerable merit with myself by asking whether the hope of these formed the highest appeal to human nature. But I overlooked an important condition which the other critics overlooked; I did not reflect that such things were shown as merely added unto those who had first sought the kingdom of God and his righteousness, and that they were no longer vicious or even so foolish when they were harmlessly come by. I have since had to own that the joys I thought trivial and sordid did rightly, as they did most strenuously, appeal to the lives hitherto starved of them. In depicting them as the common reward of the common endeavor Edward Bellamy builded better than we knew, whether he knew better or not, and he builded from a thorough sense of that level of humanity which he was destined so potently to influence,—that American level which his book found in every Christian land.

I am not sure whether this sense was ever a full consciousness with him; very possibly it was not; but in any case it was the spring of all his work, from the earliest to the latest. Somehow, whether he *knew* or not, he unerringly *felt* how the average man would feel; and all the webs of fancy that he wove were essentially of one texture through his sympathy. His imagination was intensely democratic, it was inalienably plebeian, even,—that is to say, humane. It did not seek distinction of expression; it never put the simplest and plainest reader to shame by the assumption of those fine-gentleman airs which abash and dishearten more than the mere literary swell can think. He would use a phrase or a word that was common to vulgarity, if it said what he meant; sometimes he sets one's teeth on edge, in his earlier stories, by his public school diction. But the nobility of the heart is never absent from his work; and he has always the distinction of self-forgetfulness in his art.

I have been interested, in recurring to his earlier work, to note how almost entirely the action passes in the American village atmosphere. It is like the greater part of his own life in this. He was not a man ignorant of other keeping. He was partly educated abroad, and he knew cities both in Europe and in America. He was a lawyer by profession, and he was sometime editor of a daily newspaper in a large town. But I

remember how, in one of our meetings, he spoke with distrust and dislike of the environment of cities as unwhole-
some and distracting, if not demoralizing (very much to the
effect of Tolstoy's philosophy in the matter), and in his short
stories his types are village types. They are often such when
he finds them in the city, but for much the greater part he
finds them in the village; and they are always, therefore, distinctively American; for we are village people far more than
we are country people or city people. In this as in everything
else we are a medium race, and it was in his sense, if not in
his knowledge of this fact, that Bellamy wrote so that there is
never a word or a look to the reader implying that he and the
writer are of a different sort of folk from the people in the
story.

Looking Backward, with its material delights, its commu-
nized facilities and luxuries, could not appeal to people on
lonely farms who scarcely knew of them, or to people in cities
who were tired of them, so much as to that immense average
of villagers, of small-town-dwellers, who had read much and
seen something of them, and desired to have them. This average, whose intelligence forms the prosperity of our literature,
and whose virtue forms the strength of our nation, is the environment which Bellamy rarely travels out of in his airiest
romance. He has its curiosity, its principles, its aspirations.
He can tell what it wishes to know, what problem will hold it,
what situation it can enter into, what mystery will fascinate
it, and what noble pain it will bear. It is by far the widest field
of American fiction; most of our finest artists work preferably
in it, but he works in it to different effect from any other. He
takes that life on its mystical side, and deals with types rather
than with characters; for it is one of the prime conditions of
the romancer that he shall do this. His people are less objec-
tively than subjectively present; their import is greater in what
happens to them than in what they are. But he never falsifies
them or their circumstance. He ascertains them with a fidelity
that seems almost helpless, almost ignorant of different people,
different circumstance; you would think at times that he had
never known, never seen, any others; but of course this is only
the effect of his art.

When it comes to something else, however, it is still with the same fidelity that he keeps to the small-town average,—the American average. He does not address himself more intelligently to the mystical side of this average in Dr. Heidenhoff's Process, or Miss Ludington's Sister, or any of his briefer romances, than to its ethical side in Equality. That book disappointed me, to be frank. I thought it artistically inferior to anything else he had done. I thought it was a mistake to have any story at all in it, or not to have vastly more. I felt that it was not enough to clothe the dry bones of its sociology with paper garments out of Looking Backward. Except for that one sublime moment when the workers of all sorts cry to the Lords of the Bread to take them and use them at their own price, there was no thrill or throb in the book. But I think now that any believer in its economics may be well content to let them take their chance with the American average, here and elsewhere, in the form that the author has given them. He felt that average so wittingly that he could not have been wrong in approaching it with all that public school exegesis which wearies such dilettanti as myself.

Our average is practical as well as mystical; it is first the dust of the earth, and then it is a living soul; it likes great questions simply and familiarly presented, before it puts its faith in them and makes its faith a life. It likes to start to heaven from home, and in all this Bellamy was of it, voluntarily and involuntarily. I recall how, when we first met, he told me that he had come to think of our hopeless conditions suddenly, one day, in looking at his own children, and reflecting that he could not place them beyond the chance of want by any industry or forecast or providence; and that the status meant the same impossibility for others which it meant for him. I understood then that I was in the presence of a man too single, too sincere, to pretend that he had begun by thinking of others, and I trusted him the more for his confession of a selfish premise. He never went back to himself in his endeavor, but when he had once felt his power in the world, he dedicated his life to his work. He wore himself out in thinking and feeling about it, with a belief in the good time to come that penetrated his whole being and animated his whole purpose, but apparently with no manner of fanaticism. In fact, no one could see him, or look into his quiet, gentle face, so full of goodness, so full of common sense, without perceiving that he had reasoned to his hope for justice in the frame of things. He was indeed a most practical, a most American man, without a touch of sentimentalism in his humanity. He believed that some now living should see his dream—the dream of Plato, the dream of the first Christians, the dream of Bacon, the dream of More—come true in a really civilized society; but he had the patience and courage which could support any delay.

These qualities were equal to the suffering and the death which came to him in the midst of his work, and cut him off from writing that *one more book* with which every author hopes to round his career. He suffered greatly, but he bore his suffering greatly; and as for his death, it is told that when, toward the last, those who loved him were loath to leave him at night alone, as he preferred to be left, he asked, "What can happen to me? I can only die."

I am glad that he lived to die at home in Chicopee,—in the village environment by which he interpreted the heart of the American nation, and knew how to move it more than any other American author who has lived. The theory of those who think differently is that he simply moved the popular fancy; and this may suffice to explain the state of some people, but it will not account for the love and honor in which his name is passionately held by the vast average, East and West. His fame is safe with them, and his faith is an animating force concerning whose effect at this time or some other time it would not be wise to prophesy. Whether his ethics will keep his aesthetics in remembrance I do not know; but I am sure that one cannot acquaint one's self with his merely artistic work, and not be sensible that in Edward Bellamy we were rich in a romantic imagination surpassed only by that of Hawthorne.

Hamlin Garland (1860—1940)

Hamlin Garland describes for us, in the *Bookman* of March, 1917, his introduction to Howells. One afternoon in the spring of 1881 his eye fell on "a small volume labelled *The Undiscovered Country*, by W. D. Howells," lying on the counter of a bookstand in the post office of Osage, Iowa, and, having half an hour to wait for the mail, he picked up the book and began to read. From the very first page he "dimly perceived something new in fiction." But when the letters were distributed, he laid the book aside; and he did not finish reading the story until he moved to Boston five years later. There he heard again the name of W. D. Howells.

In 1884 Garland left his father's Wisconsin farm and traveled east to prepare himself to be a teacher; in Boston he read in the Public Library and earned a precarious living by lecturing and reviewing. When he arrived, poor and friendless, Howells had recently returned to this country after a year in Europe. His reviews of new books by John Hay, Edward Bellamy, and others, appearing in the current issues of the *Century*, announced to his readers that Howells was again interested in untried talent. The first chapter of *Silas Lapham*, published in the November, 1884, *Century*, brought Howells, according to Garland, to "the full tide of his powers" and made him the subject of conversation on all sides. In fact, Garland soon discovered that Howells had become something like "a literary issue" in the clubs, newspaper offices, and drawing rooms Garland himself had begun to frequent. "All literary Boston was divided into three parts," Garland reported—those who read Howells and liked him, those who read Howells and disliked him, and those who hated Howells without reading him.

Garland found himself in the third group and did not hesitate to attack "this fictional iconoclast" in his public lectures because of Howells' reputation as an antiromantic. However, after Garland "studied to improve [his] case" and actually read *A Lady of the Aroostook, A Modern Instance, A Wom-*

an's Reason, Silas Lapham, and all the other volumes on the lengthening shelf of Howells fiction, he became not only a convert to the cause of realism but Howells' devoted disciple and "public advocate." This attitude of enthusiastic admiration marked Garland's many comments on Howells for the rest of his life. It was Garland, indeed, who proposed the toast at Howells' eightieth birthday dinner in 1917, "To William Dean Howells, dean of us all!"

Garland did not exaggerate when in his *Bookman* article he called his meeting with Howells in June, 1887,[15] "the most important literary event" of his life, for it was a long and sympathetic conversation held with Howells at this time that led to the writing of Garland's most important work, *Main-Travelled Roads,* in 1891. Before his visit with Howells in Auburndale, near Boston, Garland had published only a few poems and descriptive sketches. Howells listened to the younger man's literary dreams and encouraged him to give up his lecturing. He advised him to go back to South Dakota, where his parents were then living, and write stories of his own life. "Whatever you do, keep to the West," Howells admonished.

Though as a boy Garland had read Eggleston's *Hoosier Schoolmaster* with eager delight, he had not thought of himself as a chronicler of his own drab Western surroundings. Soon after his talk with Howells, however, he returned to South Dakota, helped on his father's farm, and began to write of the treeless plains, the boxlike houses, and the barbed-wire fences, which he saw with a new clarity. "The ugliness, the endless drudgery, and the loneliness of the farmer's lot smote me with stern insistence. I was the militant reformer." The result of Garland's indignation was a collection of stories that has become a classic in our literature, *Main-Travelled Roads.*

The book was instantly recognized by Howells and acclaimed from "The Editor's Study" of September, 1891. In his review of this "robust and terribly serious" book, Howells declared that

> these stories are full of the bitter and burning dust, the foul and trampled slush of the common avenues of life: the life of the men who hopelessly and cheerlessly make the wealth

that enriches the alien and the idler, and impoverishes the
producer. . . . The stories are full of those gaunt, grim, sordid, pathetic, ferocious figures . . . whose blind groping for
fairer conditions is so grotesque to the newspapers and so
menacing to the politicians.

Main-Travelled Roads marked the high standard that Garland set for himself and never again attained, for he was in-
capable of keeping to his chosen path. He tells us that after his
first visit with Howells, he called on him as often as he dared,
to discuss his social ideas and his literary plans. After one such
meeting Howells stood with his visitor at the garden gate and,
with a wave of the hand, said, "There lies your path." "Alas!"
added Garland in his retelling of the episode in 1917, "how
far I have fallen short of the aspirations which filled my heart
at that moment!" Garland the farm boy, self-educated too
late, was unable to sort out the eagerly seized ideas that he
had discovered in the Boston Public Library, and hence lost
the way marked out for him by his first book.

Howells remembered, in his 1912 essay on Garland, here
reprinted, that Garland, when he first called on him in
1887, was "preaching Georgism equally with veritism in
the same generous self-forgetfulness." Howells, who had already found his own path amid conflicting literary and economic ideologies, did not fall into step with Garland in his
views of "veritism," a word that Garland borrowed, he tells
us, from Eugène Véron's *Aesthetics*. The two men continued
to discuss economic as well as literary questions during the
two years, 1889-1891, that Howells and Garland were both
in Boston. Their discussions were enlarged by their association during those years with Bellamy's Nationalist Club
and the Christian Socialists.

How far Garland was influenced by his older, more experienced monitor, how far he departed from him and discerned
a new dimension in the word "realism," can be determined by
comparing Howells' *Criticism and Fiction* (1891) with Garland's *Crumbling Idols* (1894), which, we discover, differ
from one another more in emotional tone than in critical
ideas. Garland does not define veritism, for example, with any
exactness: instead, he casts around realism a romantic aura

and calls it veritism. "The veritist," he says, "is really an optimist, a dreamer. He sees life in terms of what it might be, as
well as in terms of what it is; but he writes of what is, and, at
his best, suggests what is to be by contrast."

An "optimist" and "a dreamer" who adopts economic cure-
all theories becomes a preacher in spite of his belief, shared
with the more sober realist, that a novelist's duty is to present the concrete incident, not to moralize it. Garland's "fine
courage to leave a fact with the reader, ungarnished and un-
varnished," Howells recognized and applauded in his 1891
review of *Main-Travelled Roads*; when Garland seemed to
have lost this adherence to "the fact" in his later novels full of
partially assimilated economic theory, Howells merely re-
frained from reviewing them, even though *A Spoil of Office*
(1891) was dedicated to him as "The Foremost Historian of
Our Common Lives and the Most Vital Figure in Our Literature."

That Garland was able to resist preaching in his stories as
well as he did was due, he tells us, "in large measure to Howells, who taught me to exemplify, not to preach." In letters,
conversations, and reviews Howells also attempted to curb
Garland's romantic tendency—always dangerously associated
with his didactic impulse—but without success. In his introduction to Garland's novel *They of the High Trails* (1916),
Howells mildly remarked that "we own we enjoyed the level
footing more and got our breath better in the lower altitudes
of *Main-Travelled Roads*," where Howells and Garland first
met. "Be true to the dream of thy youth—the dream of an absolute and unsparing veritism," Howells cautioned Garland in
1910. Whether Howells felt that his younger friend did in
fact remain constant to "his old young ideal of veritism" may
be studied in Howells' 1912 account of "Mr. Garland's
Books."

MR. GARLAND'S BOOKS*

The life of any man of letters who has lived long with strong
convictions becomes part of the literary history of his time,

though the history may never acknowledge it. Or, if the reader will not allow so much as this, then we may agree that inevitably such an author's life becomes bound up with that of his literary contemporaries, especially his younger contemporaries. He must have been friends or foes with nearly all of them; in the wireless of print, whether he ever met them otherwise or not, he must have exchanged with them flashes of reciprocity or repulsion, electrical thrills, which remain memories after they have ceased to be actual experiences. Shall I own at once that in this abstract case some such relation was concrete in me and the author of these admirable books; that he is the younger contemporary and I the man of letters who has lived long with strong convictions?

I suppose we were friends in the beginning, and never foes, because he had strong convictions too, and they were flatteringly like mine. When first we met, twenty years ago or more, in a pleasant suburb of Boston, there was nothing but common ground between us, and our convictions played over it together as freely and affectionately as if they had been fancies. He was a realist to the point of idealism, and he was perhaps none the less, but much the more, realist because he had not yet had time to show his faith by his works. I mean his inventive works, for he was already writing radiant criticism in behalf of what he called veritism,[16] a word he had borrowed, with due thanks, from a French critic whom he was reading with generous devotion and talking into any body who would hear him. There were as yet only a few years between him and the Wisconsin farm which grew him as genuinely as if he had been a product of its soil. He was as poor as he was young, but he was so rich in purpose of high economic and social import that he did not know he was poor. Some day, perhaps, he will himself tell the tale of that struggle to make both ends meet, the artistic and the economic ends, in those Boston days, and by teaching and lecturing to earn the time that he wished to spend in literature. He gladly wrote in the Boston newspapers for nothing, and in the best of them he was given the free hand which was far better for his future than a conditioned salary could have been. As to his present,

* From the *North American Review,* October, 1912.

he was such an ardent believer in Henry George's plan for abolishing poverty that with his heart and hopes fixed on a glorious tomorrow for all men he took no thought of his own narrow day.

He seems at that time to have gone about preaching Georgism equally with veritism in the same generous self-forgetfulness. A large public, much more intelligent than the public which reads novels instead of listening to lectures, already knew him, but I was never of this worthier public so far as hearing him speak was concerned, while we continued of the same thinking about fiction. When we both left Boston and came to New York, neither of us experienced that mental expansion, not to call it distension, which is supposed to await the provincial arriving in the metropolis; we still remained narrow-mindedly veritistic. This possibly was because we were both doubly provincial, being firstly Middle Westerners, and secondarily Bostonians, but for whatever reason it was he had already begun to show his faith by his works, in those severely conscientious studies of Wisconsin life, which I should not blame the reader for finding the best of his doing in fiction. But it is not necessary to make any such restriction in one's liking in order to vouch one's high sense of the art and the fact in *Main-Travelled Roads* and *Other Main-Travelled Roads*. The volumes are happily named: these highways are truly the paths that the sore feet of common men and women have trodden to and fro in the rude new country; they are thick with the dust and the snow of fierce summers and savage winters. I do not say but they lead now and then through beautiful springtimes and mellow autumns; they mostly seek the lonely farmers, but sometimes they tarry in sociable villages where youth and love have their dances. I do not think that I am wrong in taking "The Return of the Private" and "Up the Coolly" for types of the bare reality prevailing with the hot pity which comes from the painter's heart for the conditions he depicts.

At the time he was telling these grim stories of farm life in the West—that is, in the later years of his Boston sojourn—our author was much in contact with that great and sincere talent James A. Hearne, whom it was a dramatic education to know.[17] So far as one influenced the other I do not think

Mr. Garland owed more to Hearne than Hearne to him in practising in their art the veritism which they both preached. If I may confess a dreadful secret, I suspected them both at that time of being unconsciously romantic at heart, and only kept to reality because they did not know unreality. Hearne, in spite of such cunningest pieces of excelling nature as "Margaret Fleming" and "Drifting Apart," was often tempted to do the thing that was not—beautifully not, as Mr. James might say—in his other plays, and was willing to please his public with it, for of course the thing that is not will mainly please any public. I have no doubt the author of these books did very greatly help to stay the dramatist in his allegiance to the thing that was, while on his part Hearne doubtless helped his younger friend to clarify his native dramatic perception. At any rate, some plays relating to the nearer and farther West which Mr. Garland wrote[18] in the heyday of his Hearne friendship (it lasted to the end of the great player's life) may have been inspired by his association with a man who was to the heart of his true humanity essentially representative. As both were secretly romantic a little, so both were openly idyllic a good deal. Of course Mr. Garland's treatment of country life is more direct, more authentic, more instructive, and there is pretty sure always to be a thrill or a throe of indignant compassion in it which the milder poet did not impart to his hearers. Some plays which the novelist wrote at this time (notably "Under the Lion's Paw," a tragedy of Far Western farming) expressed this compassion, still more directly and explicitly than the stories of *Main-Travelled Roads,* and I believe it the loss of our theatre that they have never got upon the stage.

But no doubt fortune that kept him to the story written to be read was not so unintelligent as her enemies might like to imagine. In the invention of such a group of novels as *Rose of Dutcher's Coolly, The Eagle's Heart, Hesper, The Captain of the Gray-Horse Troop, Money Magic,* and *Cavanagh* he has justified the constancy of purpose which the fickle goddess has shown in his case. She seems to have known what she was about in guiding his talent from West to Farther West, from the farms to the wilds, and liberating it to the freer and bolder adventure which he must always have loved.

If the work seems to lose at times in closeness of texture on its westering way, it gains in breadth. The workman does not change in it; he is always what he was: mindful of his own past, and tenderly loyal to the simplest life, as embracing not only the potentialities but the actualities of beauty, of sublimity.

Mr. Garland's books seem to me as indigenous, in the true sense, as any our country has produced. They are western American, it is true, but America is mostly western now. But that is a question apart from the question of the author's literature. I for my part find this wholesome and edifying: I like being in the company of a man who believes so cordially in man's perfectibility; who believes that wrongs can really be righted, and that even in our depraved conditions, which imply selfishness as the greatest personal good, teaches that generosity and honesty and duty are wiser and better things. I like stirring adventure without bloodshed, as I find it so often in these pages; I like love which is sweet and pure, chivalry which is in its senses, honor for women which recognizes that while all women ultimately are good and beautiful some women are better and beautifuler than others, and some are more foolish and potentially vile enough to keep the balance of the virtues even between the sexes.

This brings me to the question of something in the author's work which I suppose has given question of its advantage to other readers as well as myself. It is something which deals with character rather than incident, and has nothing of that bad allure of so much modern fiction in its dances of the seven veils. It puts the gross passions, the propensities to shame, rather than flatters or entices them; but it doesn't recognize the beast in the man's desire of the woman, the satyr leer which is the complement of the lover's worship. In *Rose of Dutcher's Coolly,* in *Hesper,* in *Money Magic,* measurably in them all, you find the refusal, when it comes to the fact, to ignore what cannot be denied. I am old-fashioned, and I have moments when I could wish that the author had not been of such unsparing conscience. That is all, and with this wish noted I can give myself to the entire pleasure which the purity and wholesomeness of his fiction offers me.

There is an apparent want of continuity in his work. He has

ventured from the open day at times into the mystical regions
of old night, but the books here are an unbroken series in
which the average West and Far West may behold itself as in
a mirror. There is throughout, and in spite of everything, a
manly and hopeful belief in the perfectibility of man and
things. Indians, soldiers, woods, water, he teaches me that
they may all be considered to the national advantage. He does
not allow me to despair of the hero, even of the heroine; he
finds me new sorts of these in every sort of people and persuades me that they may still be naturally and charmingly in
love with one another. He paints me a West in which the
physiognomy of the East has put on new expression, kindlier,
gentler, truer, he makes me imagine a life out there which
has been somehow pacified and humbled and exalted as an escape from death and restored in gratitude to new usefulness
in that new air on that new earth. He holds me with his story
and he will not let me go till he has taught me something more
than he has told me. Greater than this I do not think we
ought to ask of any, and if we do I am sure we shall not get it.

At the end of my praise I feel that I should leave it largely
unspoken if I did not specify the power with which certain
characters and characteristics are enforced in this book and
in that. With some hesitancy I choose *Money Magic* as possibly the most masterly of the author's books. More than any
other since the stories of *The Main-Travelled Roads,* it expresses constancy to his old young ideal of veritism. He has
not hesitated to take clay from the "rude breast of the unex-
hausted West," and he has molded it in shapes which breathe
as with a life of their own like Bertha and Mart Haney (Mar-
shall Haney); she the young, beautiful wife and he an old
broken gambler, are heroine and hero on their own plane,
where they may stand with the creations of great modern fiction. The make as well as the manner of the uneducated girl,
derived from New England and bred on the frontier, but not
with all her slang and Far Western freedom underbred, is not
more credibly portrayed than the rough Irishman who has
outlived the saloon-keeper and desperado and has re-entered
as it were into the primitive goodness of his generous nature.
In both the power and the meaning of vast wealth is studied,
what it can and what it cannot do, as I do not remember to

have found it studied before. They seem the witnesses of its magic, rather than sorcerers who work it. The situation is most interesting, and the situation in Mr. Garland's book is what interests me more than the action; if I can know what people are, rather than what they do, I am the more content; and I have noted with the satisfaction which I should like to have others feel the clear conditioning of his people. In fact, his people mainly derive their importance from that. A given book of his does not present a problem for this or that character to solve it; it describes a condition which shall test him. Sometimes it is an unfriendly condition, sometimes not; but the business is to show how he copes with it. In *Money Magic,* in *The Captain of the Gray-Horse Troop*, in *Cavanagh*, in *Hesper,* in *The Eagle's Heart*, it is always a sense of the conditions which remains with me. I remember the persons from them as I learned to recognize the persons from them in their full meaning. Perhaps this is so in the novels of others, but I do not think it is, and I consider Mr. Garland's novels for this reason particularly valuable as materials of social history, no less than as very entertaining personal history. One cannot read them (and if you begin on them you *must* read them) without becoming more and more convinced that it is our conditioning which determines our characters, even though it does not always determine our actions. The strong man, the good woman, grows stronger and better for the struggle with them, though I am not sure that this is what Mr. Garland is conscious of seeking to show. I dare say that he paints them and cannot help painting them, because in his own career he has been passionately sensible of their stress even when he has not mastered all their meaning. As a singularly American artist, too, he instinctively devotes himself to the portrayal of conditions because America itself is all a novel condition.

Stephen Crane (1871—1900)

> The one thing that deeply pleases me in my literary life— brief and inglorious as it is—is the fact that men of sense believe me to be sincere. "Maggie," published in paper covers, made me the friendship of Hamlin Garland and W. D. Howells, and the one thing that makes my life worth living in the midst of all this abuse and ridicule is the consciousness that never for an instant have those friendships at all diminished.

Thus wrote Stephen Crane to Joseph O'Connor, literary editor of the Rochester *Post-Express,* on April 18, 1900, from England where he had gone to escape the outcry against *Maggie.* Early in the following June, Crane died of tuberculosis in the Black Forest, Germany.

In *Roadside Meetings* Garland tells the story of his introduction to Crane in the summer of 1891, when he was lecturing on "The Local Novel" at a summer hotel in Avon-by-the-Sea, New Jersey. After the lecture, Crane, a young reporter for the New York *Tribune,* asked to see the speaker's manuscript. Though Garland was not particularly impressed by the "slim boyish" reporter, "with sallow complexion, and light hair," he was struck by the correctness of the report that appeared the next day. The two met several times later, but more "to pass ball" and to discuss pitching than to talk about literature. Garland had all but forgotten his younger friend when, in March, 1892, he received through the mail a yellow paper-bound volume called *Maggie, A Girl of the Streets,* by "Johnstone Smith." Across the cover, in Crane's clear script, was written: "The reader of this book must inevitably be shocked, but let him keep on till the end, for in it the writer has put something which is important."

Needless to say, Garland was not shocked; instead he secured Crane's address—he was then living in New York at The Art Students' League on East Twenty-third Street—and invited him to dinner. Crane, "pale and thin," soon appeared on

Garland's doorstep, confessed his authorship of *Maggie,* and told him the story of the unsold copies of the small book, which had been privately printed with money borrowed from Crane's older brother. Garland urged Crane to mail a copy to Howells, who in the stress of his own writing and editing was not able to read the story for several weeks. Howells recalled the incident in a letter to Crane's wife, written to her after the death of her husband:

> Hamlin Garland first told me of "Maggie," which your husband then sent me. I was slow in getting at it, and he wrote me a heartbreaking note to the effect that he saw that I did not care for his book. On this I read it, and found that I did care for it immensely. I asked him to come and see me, and he came to tea and stayed far into the evening, talking about his work, and the stress that was on him to put in the profanities which I thought would shock the public from him, and about the semi-savage poor, whose type he had studied in that book.

No doubt Crane told Howells of the miserable evening he had spent the year before with Richard Watson Gilder, editor of the *Century,* who had turned down the manuscript of *Maggie* because of the "damns and the curse yehs." Howells, for his part, encouraged Crane to publish his work. In an essay on Frank Norris in the *North American Review* of December, 1902, Howells recalls these conversations with Crane. "It was interesting to hear him defend what he had written, in obedience to his experience of things, against any charge of convention. 'No,' he would contend, in behalf of the profanities of his people, 'that is the way they *talk*. I have thought of that, and whether I ought to leave such things out, but if I do I am not giving the thing as I *know* it.' "

Mildred Howells, in *Life in Letters,* tells us that her father continued to do all that he could to help launch Crane, himself taking *Maggie* from publisher to publisher. Equally important to the younger man were the conversations he held with Howells in his apartment overlooking Central Park. "William Dean Howells leaned his cheek upon the two outstretched fingers of his right hand and gazed thoughtfully at the window—the panes black from the night without, although studded once or twice with little electric stars far up on the west side of the Park." Thus Crane begins his report of a discursive talk with Howells for the October 28, 1894, issue of *The New York Times*. On one occasion Howells read Emily Dickinson's poetry aloud to his visitor. On another evening he presented Crane to dinner guests at his home with the remark, "Here is a writer who has sprung into life fully armed." Later in the evening, when Mark Twain was under discussion, Howells observed, "Mr. Crane can do things that Clemens can't."

The things that Crane could do that struck Howells as of immense importance are analyzed by Howells in his comment on *Maggie* for "Life and Letters" in *Harper's Weekly*, June 8, 1895, and in his review of *The Red Badge of Courage* for the same column soon after its publication the following October. In spite of Howells' practical acumen as an editor, what he particularly commended in *Maggie* was that "it embodied perhaps the best tough dialect which has yet found its way into print." This "parlance," impossible "to cultured ears," may be heard, Howells remarked, "by any listener in the streets of certain quarters of the city" where Howells himself often strolled. Howells liked *The Red Badge* less than *Maggie*, because "the dialect does not so much convince." But here it is "the divinations of motive and experience . . . decidedly on the psychological side" which make the book worthwhile, "as an earnest of the greater things that we may hope from a new talent working upon a high level, not quite clearly as yet, but strenuously."

On the strength of the success of *The Red Badge of Courage* both in England and in the United States, *Maggie*, together with *George's Mother*, at last appeared in both countries in June, 1896. "An Appreciation by W. D. Howells" was added to the London edition; this "Appreciation" was expanded for the New York *World* of July 26, 1896, and published under the rather journalistic title, "New York Low Life in Fiction."

On July 30, before Crane went to report the Greco-Turkish War for the New York *Journal* and the *Westminster Gazette*,

Howells sent him "this notice of your last book." Howells saw no more of Crane, for the next year he was in Cuba, reporting the Spanish-American War for the New York *World*. He returned to New York in 1899 to meet the meaningless "abuse and ridicule" that made him decide to leave the country permanently in December, 1899. Crane lived in England until he went to Germany in a futile attempt to regain his health.

In a presentation copy of *The Red Badge of Courage*, dated August 17, 1896, is the following inscription in Crane's hand: "To W. D. Howells this small and belated work as a token of veneration and gratitude of Stephen Crane for the many things he has learned of the common man and, above all, for a certain re-adjustment of his point of view victoriously concluded some time in 1892."

We know that Crane was familiar with Howells' little volume, *Criticism and Fiction*, published in May, 1891, since from this book Garland quoted his definition of realism in the lecture that Crane reported the following summer. Howells' repeated insistence on "truth" as the basis of "art," expressed so fully in *Criticism and Fiction*, is restated by Crane in these words: "To keep close to my honesty is my supreme ambition." Referring back to this period in his life, Crane wrote in 1896:

> I developed all alone a little creed of art which I thought was a good one. Later I discovered that my creed was identical with the one of Howells and Garland and in this way I became involved in the beautiful war between those who say that art is men's substitute for nature and we are most successful in art when we approach the nearest to nature and truth, and those who say—well, I don't know what they say . . . they fight villainously and keep Garland and I [sic] out of the big magazines. Howells, of course, is too powerful for them.

The "re-adjustment" of his point of view surely had something to do with Crane's discovery, in the summer of 1891, that his quest for truth was not such a bitterly lonely one as he had supposed. Howells frequently announced that he was fighting for realism, and Garland insisted that he believed in veritism; Crane might have preferred the word naturalism, made familiar by Zola's *Experimental Novel* (1880). All three were engaged in "the beautiful war" and did not quarrel over terminology. "I decided," wrote Crane, "that the nearer a writer gets to life, the greater he becomes as an artist, and most of my prose writings have been towards the goal partially described by that misunderstood and abused word, realism." When Howells asserted in *Criticism and Fiction* that "in the whole range of fiction" he knew of "no true picture of life—that is, of human nature—which is not also a masterpiece of literature," he made room for "the little tragedy," *Maggie*, which came to him in the mail the following year from an unknown young journalist.

In this review, which was mainly concerned with Stephen Crane, Howells included special praise for *Yekl, a story of the New York Ghetto,* by Abraham Cahan (1860-1951). In his *Autobiography* (1926—1931), Cahan tells us that Howells gave this story its name and himself peddled the manuscript from publisher to publisher until at last Appleton accepted it. Cahan had been a devoted follower of Howells since at least as far back as 1889, when he addressed the New York Labor Lyceum on the subject of "Realism" *(Workman's Advocate,* April 6, 1889). Citing Howells, along with Tolstoy, Turgenev, and the Russian painter Vereshchagin, as one who "paints from nature," he praised the "realistic instinct" of Howells. In the essay before us, Howells, on his part, tells of his pleasure in Cahan's fiction and expresses his conviction that Cahan is "a writer of foreign birth who will do honor to American letters," because he reflects the sights and speech of an area of New York life well known to him. He concludes by saying of Cahan's English, "In its simplicity and its purity, as the English of a man born to write Russian, it is simply marvelous."

Cahan, like Crane, "decided that the nearer a writer gets to life, the greater he becomes as an artist." Howells recognized that these younger writers were enlarging the meaning of his own concept of realism by their exploration of "low life" in East Side New York. Both Crane and Cahan were, indeed, forerunners of the naturalism soon made familiar to Ameri-

can readers by the novels of Frank Norris and Theodore
Dreiser.

NEW YORK LOW LIFE IN FICTION*

It is a long time since I have seen the once famous and popular play "A Glance at New York,"[19] but I distinctly recall
through the misty substance of some forty-five very faded
years the heroic figures of the volunteer fireman and his
friends, who were the chief persons of the piece. I do not remember the others at all, but I remember Mose, and Sikesy,
and Lize. Good and once precious fragments of the literature
linger in my memory, as: " 'Mose,' says he, 'git off o' dem
hose, or I'll swat you over der head wid der trumpet.' And I
didn't get off o' der hose, and he did swat me over der head
wid der trumpet." Other things have gone, things of Shakespeare, of Alfieri, of Cervantes, but these golden words of a
forgotten dramatist poet remain with me.

It is interesting to note that the first successful attempt to
represent the life of our streets was in dramatic form. Some
actor saw and heard things spoken with the peculiar swagger and whopper-jaw[20] utterance of the b'hoy of those
dreadful old days, when the blood-tubs and the plug-uglies
reigned over us, and Tammany was still almost purely American, and he put them on the stage and spread the poison of
them all over the land, so that there was hardly anywhere a
little blackguard boy who did not wish to act and talk like
Mose.

The whole piece was painted with the large brush and the
vivid pigments of romanticism, and yet the features were
real. So it was many long years later when Mr. Harrigan
came to the study of our low life in his delightful series of
plays. He studied it in the heyday of Irish supremacy, when
Tammany had become almost purely Celtic, and he naturally
made his heroes and heroines Irish. The old American
b'hoy[21] lingered among them in the accent and twist of an

* The *New York World,* July 26, 1896.

occasional barkeeper, but the brogue prevailed, and the high-shouldered sidelong carriage of the Americanized bouncer of Hibernian blood.

The treatment, however, was still romanticistic, though Mr. Harrigan is too much of a humorist not to return suddenly to nature, and at times from the most exalted regions of "imagination." He loves laughing and making laugh, and that always saved him when he was in danger of becoming too grand, or fine, or heroic. He had moments when he was exactly true, but he allowed himself a good many friendly freedoms with the fact, and the effect was not always that of reality.

It seemed to me that so far as I could get the drift of a local drama in German which flourished at one of the East Side theatres a winter ago, that the author kept no more faithfully to life than Mr. Harrigan, and had not his sublime moments of absolute fidelity. In fact, the stage is almost as slow as criticism to perceive that there is no other standard for the arts but life, and it keeps on with the conventional in motive even when the matter is honest, apparently in the hope that by doing the stale falsehood often enough it will finally affect the witness like a fresh verity. It is to the honor of the stage, however, that it was first to recognize the value of our New York low life as material; and I shall always say that Mr. Harrigan, when he was not overpowered by a tradition or a theory, was exquisitely artistic in his treatment of it. He was then true, and, as Tolstoy has lately told us, to be true is to be moral.

The fiction meant to be read, as distinguishable from the fiction meant to be represented, has been much later in dealing with the same material, and it is only just beginning to deal with it in the spirit of the great modern masters. I cannot find that such clever and amusing writers as Mr. Townsend, or Mr. Ralph, or Mr. Ford have had it on their consciences to report in the regions of the imagination the very effect of the life which they all seem at times to have seen so clearly. There is apparently nothing but the will that is wanting in either of them, but perhaps the want of the will is the want of an essential factor, though I should like very much to have them try for a constant reality in their studies; and I am far from wishing to count them out in an estimate of what has been done in that direction. It is only just to Mr. Stephen Crane, however, to say that he was first in the field where they made themselves known earlier. His story of "Maggie, a Girl of the Streets," which has been recently published by the Appletons, was in the hands of a few in an edition which the author could not even give away three years ago; and I think it is two years, now, since I saw "George's Mother," which Edward Arnold has brought out, in the manuscript.

Their present publication is imaginably due to the success of "The Red Badge of Courage"; but I do not think that they will owe their critical acceptance to the obstreperous favor which that has won. As pieces of art they are altogether superior to it, and as representations of life their greater fidelity cannot be questioned. In "The Red Badge of Courage" there is a good deal of floundering, it seems to me. The narration repeats itself; the effort to imagine, to divine, and then to express ends often in a huddled and confused effect; there is no repose, such as agony itself assumes in the finest art, and there is no forward movement. But in these other books the advance is relentless; the atmosphere is transparent; the texture is a continuous web where all the facts are wrought with the unerring mastery of absolute knowledge. I should say that "The Red Badge of Courage" owed its excellence to the training the author had given himself in setting forth the life he knew in these earlier books of later publication. He learned to imagine vividly from seeing clearly.

There is a curious unity in the spirit of the arts; and I think that what strikes me most in the story of "Maggie" is that quality of fatal necessity which dominates Greek tragedy. From the conditions it all had to be, and there were the conditions. I felt this in Mr. Hardy's "Jude," where the principle seems to become conscious in the writer; but there is apparently no consciousness of any such motive in the author of "Maggie." Another effect is that of an ideal of artistic beauty which is as present in the working out of this poor girl's squalid romance as in any classic fable. This will be foolishness, I know, to the foolish people who cannot discriminate between the material and the treatment in art, and who think that beauty is inseparable from daintiness and prettiness, but I do not speak of them. I appeal rather to such as feel them-

selves akin with every kind of human creature, and find
neither high nor low when it is a question of inevitable suffering, or of a soul struggling vainly with an inexorable fate.

My rhetoric scarcely suggests the simple terms the author
uses to produce the effect which I am trying to report again.
They are simple, but always most graphic, especially when it
comes to the personalities of the story: the girl herself, with
her bewildered wish to be right and good; with her distorted
perspective; her clinging and generous affections; her hopeless environments; the horrible old drunken mother, a cyclone
of violence and volcano of vulgarity; the mean and selfish
lover, a dandy tough, with his gross ideals and ambitions; her
brother, an Ishmaelite from the cradle, who, with his war-
like instincts beaten back into cunning, is what the b'hoy of
former times has become in our more strenuously policed
days. He is indeed a wonderful figure in a group which betrays no faltering in the artist's hand. He, with his dull hates,
his warped good-will, his cowed ferocity, is almost as fine artistically as Maggie, but he could not have been so hard to do,
for all the pathos of her fate is rendered without one maudlin touch.

So is that of the simple-minded and devoted and tedious
old woman who is George's mother in the book of that
name. This is scarcely a study at all, while Maggie is really
and fully so. It is the study of a situation merely: a poor, inadequate woman, of a commonplace religiosity, whose son
goes to the bad. The wonder of it is the courage which deals
with persons so absolutely average, and the art that graces
them with the beauty of the author's compassion for everything that errs and suffers. Without this feeling the effects of
his mastery would be impossible, and if it went further or put
itself into the pitying phrases it would annul the effects. But it
never does this; it is notable how in all respects the author
keeps himself well in hand. He is quite honest with his reader.
He never shows his characters or his situations in any sort of
sentimental glamour; if you will be moved by the sadness of
common fates you will feel his intention, but he does not flatter his portraits of people or conditions to take your fancy.

In George and his mother he has to do with folk of country
origin as the city affects them, and the son's decadence is ad-

mirably studied; he scarcely struggles against temptation, and his mother's only art is to cry and to scold. Yet he loves her, in a way, and she is devotedly proud of him. These simple country folk are contrasted with simple city folk of varying degrees of badness. Mr. Crane has the skill to show how evil is greatly the effect of ignorance and imperfect civilization. The club of friends, older men than George, whom he is asked to join, is portrayed with extraordinary insight, and the group of young toughs whom he finally consorts with is done with even greater mastery. The bulldog motive of one of them, who is willing to fight to the death, is most impressively rendered.

The student of dialect ought to be interested in the parlance of the class Mr. Crane draws upon for his characters. They are almost inarticulate; not merely the grammar, but the language itself, decays in their speech. The Theta sound, so characteristic of English, disappears altogether, and the vowels tend to lose themselves in the obscure note heard in *fur* and *stir*. What will be the final language spoken by the New Yorker? We shall always write and print a sort of literary English, I suppose, but with the mixture of races the spoken tongue may be a thing composite and strange beyond our present knowledge. Mr. Abraham Cahan, in his "Yekl, a Story of the New York Ghetto" (Appleton's), is full of indirect suggestion upon this point. Perhaps we shall have a New York jargon which shall be to English what the native Yiddish of his characters is to Hebrew, and it will be interlarded with Russian, Polish and German words, as their present jargon is with English vocables and with American slang.

Yekl is a young Russian Jew who is very anxious to be Americanized in every way, and who takes on our smartness and vulgarity with an instinctive fitness for that degree of fellow-citizenship. He is thoroughly selfish, immoral, irreligious, cunning and vain, which does not prevent his having moments of remorse and tenderness and living in a cloud of inherited superstitions. He was Yekl Podernik at home, but in Boston, where he made his first American sojourn, his zeal for our habits and customs won him the nickname of Jake the Yankee. The action of the story all passes in the region of Hester Street, where Jake works in a sweat-shop, and where he makes a home for his wife and child when they come over to him from Povodye.

As Mr. Cahan is a Russian, and as romanticism is not considered literature in Russia, his story is, of course, intensely realistic. It could not be more so indeed than Mr. Crane's stories, and it is neither more nor less faithful than these. The artistic principle which moves both writers is the same; but the picturesque, outlandish material with which Mr. Cahan deals makes a stronger appeal to the reader's fancy. He has more humor than the American, too, whose spare laughter is apt to be grim, while the Russian cannot hide his relish of the comic incidents of his story. It is mainly not at all comic, however, but tragical as the divorce of the poor little Russian wife can make it, though the reader is promptly consoled by her marriage with a man worthier of her than Jake the Yankee. He goes away and weds the Americanized "Polish snope" whom he had flirted with before his wife came out to him.

The tale is well told, with spirit and with artistic pleasure on the author's part, whose sense of character is as broad as his sense of human nature is subtle and deep. I cannot help thinking that we have in him a writer of foreign birth who will do honor to American letters, as Boyesen did. He is already thoroughly naturalized to our point of view; he sees things with American eyes and he brings in aid of his vision the far and rich perceptions of his Hebraic race; while he is strictly of the great and true Russian principle in literary art. There is much that is painful in his story, as there is much that is dreadful in Mr. Crane's work, but both of these writers persuade us that they have told the truth, and that such as conditions have made the people they deal with, we see their people. If we have any quarrel with the result we cannot blame the authors, who have done their duty as artists and for a moment have drawn aside the thick veil of ignorance which parts the comfortable few from the uncomfortable many in this city. The life they know lives before us, as we read; and the saddest thing about it is that this life as we see it after a generation of New York in Mr. Crane's stories is more hopeless than it is as we find it in Mr. Cahan's tale, which deals with the first years of his hero's contact with our civilization. Doubtless, also, temperament has something

to do with this effect. Mr. Crane is essentially tragical, and
Mr. Cahan, without being less serious, is essentially humorous. *Yekl* is, in fact, a charming book, and is not only delightful in itself but in its promise of future work. The author
who could imagine Mrs. Kavarsky, the meddlesome, amiable
neighbor of poor Githa, Jake's wife, and Mamie, "the Polish
snope," and Fanny, "the Preacher," with the scenes in the
sweat-shop, at the dancing academy and, above all, in the
Rabbi's parlor at the time of the divorce, has bound himself
by the very excellence of what he has done to do much more
that is better still.

I had almost forgotten to speak of his English. In its simplicity and its purity, as the English of a man born to write
Russian, it is simply marvelous.

Frank Norris (1870—1902)

Frank Norris spent the spring of 1898 in New York as a reader for the publishing house of *McClure's Magazine,* having been invited to join the staff on the strength of the first few installments of *Moran,* which appeared in the San Francisco *Wave* between January and April, 1898. In a small back bedroom on West Thirty-third Street, Norris was lonely, homesick, and often ill. Through Gelett Burgess he met Howells soon after his arrival and discussed with him the manuscript of his new novel, *McTeague,* on which he had been working under Lewis Edwards Gates at Harvard. On March 12, 1898, Norris wrote to a friend in San Francisco: "By the way, Mr. Burgess took me to call on Howells last Monday evening. We had a most charming visit. I find him one of the most delightful men imaginable and, as you told me, especially fond of good talk."

Howells reviewed the completed novel, *Moran of the Lady Letty,* the following December for *Literature,* commending it—in spite of its "romanticistic" atmosphere—for "being so boldly circumstanced in the light of common day, and in a time and place of our own." He reviewed *McTeague* for the March 24, 1899, issue of the same magazine, claiming for himself a "weather-wise eye," for in his earlier review he had suggested that one might expect a change in Norris' writing from the romantic to the realistic. He recognized, however, the influence of Zola, whose novels Norris had been eagerly reading at the University of California after his return from a year in Paris. In his adherence to Zola, Howells pointed out, Norris had stressed the brutal side of his story; therefore, his "true picture of life is not true, because it leaves beauty out." A mild reproof, indeed, amid the flood of reviews that stamped *McTeague* as *"repulsive," "sordid,"* and *"brutal."* In an undated letter of thanks for Howells' kind notice, Norris showed that he agreed—within limits—with his strictures and that he was "buzzing" with new ideas for a trilogy of far wider scope. This letter is the only one we have from Norris to his
212

older friend and adviser; it indicates the confidence and the respectful appreciation this vigorous exponent of the new school of naturalism felt for his elderly critic.

61 Washington Sq. S.
Tuesday

My dear Mr. Howells:

Need I say how pleased and delighted I am over your review of McTeague *in this last number of* Literature. *It has encouraged me more than anything that has ever been said of my work. I believe too, you were quite right in saying that it was not the whole truth, and that the novel that is true to life cannot afford to ignore the finer things. I agree in every one of your criticisms always excepting the anticlimax, the "death in the desert" business. I am sure that has its place. I have the idea of another novel or rather series of novels buzzing in my head these days. I think there is a chance for somebody to do some great work with the West and California as a background, and which will be at the same time thoroughly American. My idea is to write three novels around the one subject of Wheat. First, a story of California (the producer), second, a story of Chicago (the distributor), third, a story of Europe (the consumer) and in each to keep up the idea of this huge Niagara of wheat rolling from West to East. I think a big epic trilogy could be made out of such a subject, that at the same time would be modern and distinctly American. The idea is so big that it frightens me at times but I have about made up my mind to have a try at it.*

Thanking you again, Mr. Howells, for your very kind interest in my work, believe me

Very sincerely,
Frank Norris

By April, Norris had gone to California to gather his material for *The Octopus;* before leaving he discussed the plan for the trilogy with Howells "in one of those few meetings which seem, too late, as if they might have been so many," which Howells recalled a few weeks after the death of the younger man in the essay on Norris written for the *North American Review*, December, 1902. Norris' plan must have been particularly interesting to Howells, for the enormous concept was an illustration of Howells' own idea of social "complicity."

In his essay, "The Novel With a Purpose" (1901), Norris explained his technique for the sociological novel, which "draws conclusions from a whole congeries of forces, social tendencies, race impulses" and devotes itself "not to a study of men, but of man," a technique that Norris had discovered in Zola's *Experimental Novel* (1880). *The Octopus*, a milestone in American naturalistic fiction, was finally published in April, 1901; Howells reviewed it for "The Editor's Easy Chair" the following October, and welcomed "this poet among the California wheat-fields," who had written "an epic of Zolaesque largeness." Norris, said Howells, owed to the great romantic realist "nothing but the conception of treating a modern theme epically. That is what he did, as to the place, in his *McTeague*, and that is what he has done, as to the action, in *The Octopus*." The tricks of Norris' character portrayal, the melodrama of his plot, Howells deplored in his, on the whole laudatory, appraisal of "a great book, simple, sombre, large, and of a final authority as the record of a tragical passage of American, of human events."

Norris died one year after Howells' review of *The Octopus*. Howells, looking back over the astonishing career of the first genuine American naturalistic writer, remarked, "I never met him but he made me feel that he could do it, the thing he meant to do, and do it robustly and quietly." The thing he meant to do was "the great American novel." *The Pit*, published posthumously in March, 1903, and reviewed the same month by Howells in *Harper's Weekly*, became at once a best seller, almost fulfilling this hope for the readers of that decade. It is interesting to notice that the rough and powerful hero of the novel, Curtis Jadwin, considered Howells his favorite novelist when he was introduced to Howells' stories by his culture-seeking wife. "Lapham he loved as a brother," wrote Norris.

A year before his death Norris hastily composed several essays on the novel, later gathered together under the title *The Responsibilities of the Novelist*. In one, entitled "An American School of Fiction?" Norris discussed Howells. Though Norris referred to Howells' realism as "the drama of the broken teacup, the adventure of an invitation to dinner," he also observed:

> Of all producers of American fiction he has had the broadest vision, at once a New Englander and a New Yorker, an Easterner and—in the Eastern sense—a Westerner. But one swallow does not make a summer, nor does one writer constitute a "school." Mr. Howells has had no successors. Instead, just as we had with *Lapham* and *The Modern Instance* laid the foundation of fine, hardy literature, that promised to be our very, very own, we commence to build upon it a whole confused congeries of borrowed, faked, pilfered romanticisms.

Romantic follower of Zola though he was, Norris was also the successor of Howells and an admirer of *Silas Lapham* and *A Modern Instance*. *The Responsibilities of the Novelist* drew from Howells' *Criticism and Fiction* as well as from Zola's *Experimental Novel*. In one of the essays in his collection, "A Plea for Romantic Fiction," Norris carried on the familiar argument with Howells as to the meaning of realism and romance, giving his own twist to the definition of romance, to which, as a follower of Zola, he was partial:

> Now, let us understand at once what is meant by Romance and what by Realism. Romance, I take it, is the kind of fiction that takes cognizance of variations from the type of normal life. Realism is the kind of fiction that confines itself to the type of normal life. According to this definition, then, Romance may even treat of the sordid, the unlovely—as, for instance, the novels of M. Zola. (Zola has been dubbed a Realist, but he is, on the contrary, the very head of the Romanticists.) Also, Realism, used as it sometimes is as a term of reproach, need not be in the remotest sense or degree offensive, but on the other hand respectable as a church and

proper as a deacon—as, for instance, the novels of Mr. Howells.

A CASE IN POINT*

The question of expansion in American fiction lately agi-
tated by a lady novelist of Chicago[22] with more vehemence
than power, and more courage than coherence, seems to me
again palpitant in the case of a new book by a young writer,
which I feel obliged at once to recognise as altogether a remarkable book. Whether we shall abandon the old-fashioned
American ideal of a novel as something which may be read by
all ages and sexes, for the European notion of it as something
fit only for age and experience, and for men rather than wom-
en; whether we shall keep to the bounds of the provincial proprieties, or shall include within the imperial territory of our
fiction the passions and the motives of the savage world which
underlies as well as environs civilisation, are points which this
book sums up and puts concretely; and it is for the reader,
not for the author, to make answer. There is no denying the
force with which he makes the demand, and there is no denying the hypocrisies which the old-fashioned ideal of the novel
involved. But society, as we have it, is a tissue of hypocrisies,
beginning with the clothes in which we hide our nakedness,
and we have to ask ourselves how far we shall part with them
at his demand. The hypocrisies are the proprieties, the decen-
cies, the morals; they are by no means altogether bad; they
are, perhaps, the beginning of civilisation; but whether they
should be the end of it is another affair. That is what we are to
consider in entering upon a career of imperial expansion in a
region where the Monroe Doctrine was never valid. From the
very first Europe invaded and controlled in our literary world.
The time may have come at last when we are to invade and
control Europe in literature. I do not say that it has come,
but if it has we may have to employ European means and
methods.

* *Literature,* March 24, 1899.

It ought not to be strange that the impulse in this direction should have come from California, where, as I am always affirming rather than proving, a continental American fiction began. I felt, or fancied I felt, the impulse in Mr. Frank Norris' "Moran of the Lady Letty," and now in his "McTeague" I am so sure of it that I am tempted to claim the prophetic instinct of it. In the earlier book there were, at least, indications that forecast to any weather-wise eye a change from the romantic to the realistic temperature, and in the later we have it suddenly, and with the overwhelming effect of a blizzard. It is saying both too much and too little to say that Mr. Norris has built his book on Zolaesque lines, yet Zola is the master of whom he reminds you in a certain epical conception of life. He reminds you of Zola also in the lingering love of the romantic, which indulges itself at the end in an anticlimax worthy of Dickens. He ignores as simply and sublimely as Zola any sort of nature or character beyond or above those of Polk Street in San Francisco, but within the ascertained limits he convinces you, two-thirds of the time, of his absolute truth to them. He does not, of course, go to Zola's lengths, breadths, and depths; but he goes far enough to difference his work from the old-fashioned American novel.

Polite readers of the sort who do not like to meet in fiction people of the sort they never meet in society will not have a good time in "McTeague," for there is really not a society person in the book. They might, indeed, console themselves a little with an elderly pair of lovers on whom Mr. Norris wreaks all the sentimentality he denies himself in the rest of the story; and as readers of that sort do not mind murders as much as vulgarity, they may like to find three of them, not much varying in atrocity. Another sort of readers will not mind the hero's being a massive blond animal, not necessarily bad, though brutal, who has just wit enough to pick up a practical knowledge of dentistry and follow it as a trade; or the heroine's being a little, pretty, delicate daughter of German-Swiss emigrants, perfectly common in her experiences and ideals, but devotedly industrious, patient, and loyal. In the chemistry of their marriage McTeague becomes a prepotent ruffian, with always a base of bestial innocence; and Trina becomes a pitiless miser without altogether losing her housewifely virtues or ceasing to feel a woman's rapture in giving up everything but her money to the man who maltreats her more and more, and, finally, murders her.

This is rendering in coarse outline the shape of a story realized with a fulness which the outline imparts no sense of. It abounds in touches of character at once fine and free, in little miracles of observation, in vivid insight, in simple and subtle expression. Its strong movement carries with it a multiplicity of detail which never clogs it; the subordinate persons are never shabbed or faked; in the equality of their treatment their dramatic inferiority is lost; their number is great enough to give the feeling of a world revolving round the central figures without distracting the interest from these. Among the minor persons, Maria Macapa, the Mexican chorewoman, whose fable of a treasure of gold turns the head of the Polish Jew Zerkow, is done with rare imaginative force. But all these lesser people are well done; and there are passages throughout the book that live strongly in the memory, as only masterly work can live. The one folly is the insistence on the love-making of those silly elders, which is apparently introduced as an offset to the misery of the other love-making; the anti-climax is McTeague's abandonment in the alkali desert, hand-cuffed to the dead body of his enemy.

Mr. Norris has, in fact, learned his lesson well, but he has not learned it all. His true picture of life is not true, because it leaves beauty out. Life is squalid and cruel and vile and hateful, but it is noble and tender and pure and lovely, too. By and by he will put these traits in, and then his powerful scene will be a reflection of reality; by and by he will achieve something of the impartial fidelity of the photograph. In the mean time he has done a picture of life which has form, which has texture, which has color, which has what great original power and ardent study of Zola can give, but which lacks the spiritual light and air, the consecration which the larger art of Tolstoy gives. It is a little inhuman, and it is distinctly not for the walls of living-rooms, where the ladies of the family sit and the children go in and out. This may not be a penalty, but it is the inevitable consequence of expansion in fiction.

Notes to Part I: European Masters

1. See verses by Edmund Gosse deriding Howells for his attack on Dickens in an article by the present authors, "An Enchanted Guest," *Journal of the Rutgers University Library,* XXII (June, 1959).

2. *Nation,* III (December 6, 1866), 453—54.

3. Pseudonym for Klara (Müller) Mundt, 1814—1873.

4. With this essay cf. "The Editor's Study," LXXVIII (December, 1888), 158—59.

5. Discussed in "The Postmaster-General and the Censorship of Morals," *Arena,* II (October, 1890), 540—52.

6. For the "comment" see the *New York Herald,* June 22, 1890, p. 22, and the editorial "Tolstoi on Marriage," p. 16; and July 5, 1891, p. 8, for careful statements by Tolstoy concerning his attitude and the contemporary reception of his view; see also L. N. Tolstoy, "Guy de Maupassant," *Arena,* II (1894), 15—26; *New York Herald,* April 26, 1891, p. 12.

Notes to Part II: American Writers

1. Howells' memory is at fault. He became editor of the *Atlantic* in July, 1871 at the age of thirty-four, when Fields (born December 31, 1817) was still fifty-three.

2. The full names and dates of the less well-known writers whom Howells mentions are here given: Alice Cary (1820—1871), James Freeman Clarke (1810—1888), Abby Morton Diaz (1821—1904), Henry Giles (1809—1882), Annie Douglas Greene Robinson, pseudonym "Marian Douglas" (1842—1913), George Stillman Hillard

(1808—1879), Walter Mitchell (1826—1908), Fitz-James O'Brien (1828—1862), John Williamson Palmer (1825—1906), Norah Perry (1841—1896), W. J. Still (1828—1901), David A. Wasson (1823—1887), Adeline D. T. Whitney (1824—1906), Forceythe Willson (1837—1867).

3. Leonard Case (1820—1880).

4. Over and over one learns of Howells' helpfulness to young authors; see, for instance, the *New York Herald*, November 27, 1892, p. 31.

5. Howells perhaps refers to "A Light Man," which he had apparently advised James to submit to *Galaxy*, in which it appeared in July, 1869.

6. Sarah Butler Wister (1761—1804).

7. Jonas Lie (1833—1908), a well-known Norwegian writer.

8. Alexander Lange Kielland (1849—1906), Norwegian novelist.

9. Emerson's essay "The American Scholar."

10. Hiram Rich (1832—19—?).

11. William Henry Bishop (1847—1928).

12. Fiske dedicated *Myths and Myth-Makers* (1872) to Howells.

13. "L'Ecole du Flat-Creek," *Revue des Deux Mondes*, 102 (November, 1872), 125—76.

14. For a discussion of Howells and Bellamy's socialism see the *New York Herald*, September 23, 1894, section 6, p. 7. Cf. "Mr. Howells's Millenium," *American Fabian*, July, 1898, pp. 6—7.

15. Garland gives two dates for his first meeting with Howells. In "Meetings with Howells" (*Bookman*, March, 1917, p. 3), the date given is June, 1887. In "Meeting with Howells," *Roadside Meetings* (1930), pp. 55—56, the date is October, 1885. The date given in the *Bookman* is probably the more authentic because written nearer the event.

16. Garland took the word "veritism" from the French writer Eugène Véron (1825—1889) whose *Aesthetics* was translated into English by W. H. Armstrong (1879).

17. Garland reports a conversation held in 1890 between Howells and James A. Herne, *Bookman*, 45 (March,

1917), 6—7. Howells suggested to Herne that "he take a sail-loft, if necessary, and produce his new play Margaret Fleming." The result was the production of the play in Chickering Hall, Boston, in 1890. "Mr. and Mrs. Herne," *Arena*, IV (October, 1891), 543—60. According to the *New York Herald*, December 13, 1891, p. 12, "The reception of the play by the public in the modern Athens [Boston] hardly bore out Mr. W. D. Howells in his optimism."

18. One of these plays was *Under the Wheel, A Modern Play in Six Scenes* (1890).

19. *A Glance at New York*, by Benjamin Archibald Baker, produced in 1848.

20. In *The Minister's Charge*, p. 84, Howells defines this word, which is not found in his sense in dictionaries: "She was what they call whopper-jawed, and spoke a language almost purely consonantal, cutting and clipping her words with a rapid play of her whopper-jaw till there was nothing but the bare bones left of them." "E. A." questioned Howells' usage and definition of the word. *Critic*, V (1886), 238.

21. *b'hoy*, a tough character or rowdy; *blood-tubs*, a gang of roughs formerly active in Baltimore; *plug-uglies*, members of a gang of rowdies and ruffians formerly active in Baltimore, New York, and Philadelphia.

" 'Blood-tubs and plug-uglies, and others galore,
Are sick for a thrashing in sweet Baltimore.' "

—Dictionary of American English.

22. This was Lilian Lida Bell (later Mrs. A. H. Bogue), 1865—1929, whose address to the Chicago Baptist Social Union was reported in *The New York Times*, February 19, 1899, p. 13, and the *Critic*, XXXI (1899), 310—11. Howells remarked on it in "Problems of Existence in Fiction," *Literature*, March 10, 1899 (see p. 275 in this book).